MICHIGAN LABOR
A Brief History from
1818 to the Present

MICHIGAN LABOR
A Brief History from
1818 to the Present

Doris B. McLaughlin

ANN ARBOR
INSTITUTE OF LABOR AND INDUSTRIAL RELATIONS
THE UNIVERSITY OF MICHIGAN—WAYNE STATE UNIVERSITY
1970

Michigan Labor: A Brief History from 1818 to the Present
Copyright © 1970
by the Institute of Labor and Industrial Relations,
The University of Michigan—Wayne State University
All rights reserved
LCCN: 73-633304   ISBN: 0-87736-312-9
Printed in the United States of America

All Americans have a vital stake in the shaping of sound
public and private industrial relations policies and in the
expansion of pertinent knowledge and skills. The Institute
of Labor and Industrial Relations is a joint agency of
The University of Michigan (Ann Arbor) and Wayne State
University (Detroit). It was established in the spring of
1957 in order to maximize the contribution of each University, in activities related to industrial relations, to the
people of Michigan, and to the educational and research
needs of workers and management.

The Institute has three major functions: first, to facili-
tate regular university instruction in the disciplines and
professions related to industrial relations; second, to encourage basic and applied research on industrial relations
topics; and third, to organize and promote programs of
community education in industrial relations designed to
serve labor, management, and the public.

Charles M. Rehmus

Co-Director
The University of Michigan
Ann Arbor

Ronald W. Haughton

Co-Director
Wayne State University
Detroit

FOREWORD

For those who date Michigan's trade union movement from the struggles of the industrial workers in the 1930s, this book will put the record in proper perspective, for it recounts the story of the previous 100 years, when many of today's programs were tried and tested. I, for one, had known almost nothing about labor's struggles during the lumbering days in the Saginaw Valley.

It is interesting to note, too, that such early Michigan labor leaders as Richard Trevellick fully realized the relationship between collective bargaining goals and political action. Trevellick's approach to political activity is not unlike labor's current role—with, of course, some modifications. The independent political role which Trevellick tried and which was eventually discarded because it proved ineffective was also proposed by some of the pioneer leaders of industrial unionism in the 1930s and early 1940s. In the end, the present policy of working within the basic structure of the two-party system has proved more successful than trying to establish a separate labor party.

I can understand the feeling against the political establishment on the part of some of us who had to engage in sit-downs and participate in other similar struggles in the 1930s to win the right to join a union. However, labor has learned that it must have allies—especially in the political arena—to achieve its goals. The Michigan political experience—where labor scored landmark improvements in labor legislation in the 1965-66 session of the state legislature—supports the basic soundness of this approach.

I was pleased that the author chose the struggle of the Upper Peninsula copper miners for treatment as a full chapter in the book. Next to the struggles of the 1930s in the auto industry, I feel that the battle of the copper miners was Michigan labor's finest hour. The auto industry dominated the worker's life before the organizing drives. In the Upper Peninsula copper mines, the owners also claimed title to the worker's homes and managed his entire life. The violence used against the Western

v

Federation of Miners during the lengthy strike was a forerunner of the repressive tactics that the fledgling CIO auto union and other industrial unions were to face some twenty years later.

As an addendum to Chapter 3 on Battle Creek, let me point out that the cereal workers involved in it are now represented by the American Grain Millers, an effective and community minded labor union.

I must also concur with the author's decision to devote an entire chapter to labor's modern role in Michigan politics, and another to the growth of public employee unions. Labor's detractors often misrepresent trade union involvement in the political arena. It is gratifying to see labor's political activity treated as it is in this book. I also appreciate the section on the fight for "one man, one vote" at the ballot box—a struggle in which I was involved and which I feel is the most important gain since the adoption of the original U.S. Constitution and Bill of Rights. Public employee and service unions are the wave of the future in the labor movement. Again, the role of Michigan labor was a key one in winning passage of the public employee collective bargaining law.

This book is a valuable addition to the sparse material now available to our schools and libraries and should be of interest to anyone who wishes to know something about Michigan labor's heritage.

August 1970

> AUGUST SCHOLLE
> President
> Michigan AFL-CIO

PREFACE

This brief book is intended as an introduction to the history of organized labor in Michigan, and touches only the more significant highlights of the story. There is much more to tell, and it is hoped that someday someone will fill in the gaps.

This work owes a great deal to many people, and I would like to take this opportunity to thank them. Professor Charles Rehmus, Ann Arbor Co-Director of the Institute of Labor and Industrial Relations, encouraged me to undertake the work, found the funds to underwrite it, and made innumerable valuable suggestions that have made the finished product a better work.

The staff at The University of Michigan libraries and particularly those persons connected with the Labadie Collection, Rare Book Room, and Bureau of Government Library were most cooperative. The Michigan Historical Collections people cheerfully went out of their way to direct me to materials I needed, as did the librarian at the Michigan Municipal League.

Professor Jacqueline Brophy of the Michigan State University School of Labor and Industrial Relations read the entire manuscript with great care. Her comments reflected her keen interest in and thorough knowledge of American labor history and were extremely helpful.

A number of others also read some or all of the manuscript. These included persons active in the labor movement, members of the academic community, friends, family—and a long-suffering husband. To list them all would require more space than is available, but I hope they know that this does not lessen my debt to them. The suggestions they had to offer made a positive contribution to this work. The faults are all my own.

August 1970

Doris B. McLaughlin

CONTENTS

ILLUSTRATIONS

Chapter 6

Chapter 7

MICHIGAN LABOR
A Brief History from 1818 to the Present

Detroit in 1820, a lithograph of the 1870s copied from a contemporary watercolor by General Alexander Macomb. The large ship in the middle is *Walk-in-the-Water*, the first steam-powdered vessel on the Great Lakes, which carried many of the early settlers to Michigan.

1

BACKGROUND

Until the early years of the nineteenth century, mapmakers described Michigan as "interminable swamp." That dismal label was rarely disputed, since few Americans had ever visited the remote region between the Great Lakes. Until the outbreak of the War of 1812, the area remained primarily the province of the fur trader and the Indian. An occasional army outpost with a small settlement huddled around it provided virtually the only evidence that "civilization" had arrived. As late as 1810 Detroit, the most populous community in the Michigan Territory, was a village of 750 inhabitants.

The picture changed after the War of 1812. The area had served as a major battleground during the conflict, and the government in Washington now recognized its strategic value. Construction began in 1818 on military roads linking Detroit with the tiny settlement of Chicago and with the Ohio Valley. Moreover, a number of men who had come to the Territory on military duty decided to settle there after the war. Their letters to family and friends, along with the road surveyors' reports and other accounts, corrected earlier impressions of Michigan's potential as an area for settlement. As public interest in the region heightened, the federal government took steps to clear the region of Indians. The Ottawas, Chippewas, and Potawatomi were gradually driven further north and west. As they moved out, settlers moved in.

Steamships began plying the Great Lakes in 1818 and shortened travel time from the East—an added factor in attracting settlers. By then a slow but steady flow of people was moving to the Michigan Territory.

Normally they came by ship and landed in Detroit—then, as now, the most important commercial center in Michigan. The 1818 arrival found himself in a town of just over a thousand inhabitants, crowded into 142 dwellings. There were no sidewalks, and the streets were unpaved. When it rained, the roads were cluttered with carts stuck in the mud. An open drain served as the town's sewer system, and early antipollution forces complained bitterly of the smell and the filth. Residents were no happier with their water supply. They contended that it was so contaminated that it constituted a health menace. Its foul taste led one man to counsel that "those whose principles forbid disguising water with brandy will be constrained to drink beer."

But better days were ahead. Public works and new housing were underway in Detroit, and roads, bridges, and canals were being built to connect it with the surrounding area. Because of the construction boom, labor was much in demand—a marked contrast to the eastern labor market, which was still feeling the effects of the depression following the War of 1812. Many of the newcomers were attracted to Michigan because jobs were plentiful and wages high. Skilled workers received anywhere from $1.50 to $2.25 a day, and common laborers averaged $1.00. At the time, artisans in the East were earning a daily wage of between $.84 and $1.34, and the unskilled made as little as twelve and a half cents. But high wages in Detroit were offset by high prices, because many commodities still had to be imported from the East; and local transport from the developing agricultural area around Detroit was also costly because the few connecting roads were in poor condition. A contemporary Detroit newspaper complained that the cost of living was higher there than anywhere else in the country.

A number of the newly arrived workers purchased land near Detroit and combined farming with their other vocation. By doing so, they saved money on the cost of food and could supplement their incomes by selling their surplus crops. It was still possible, and often necessary, to be both farmer and wage earner. The towns were small, and the number of potential consumers limited. In the early decades of the nineteenth century "industrial activity" in the largest towns—Detroit, Monroe, Pontiac—was largely limited to the production of items for local consumption such as leather, flour, woolens, lumber, candles, and soap. Other articles were normally made to order by a master craftsman working at home or in a small shop with, at most, a handful of journeymen and apprentices. Rarely were these full-time occupations. In order to tap a mass market and operate year-round, factories required more extensive transportation facilities than Michigan could offer.

The new arrivals, long familiar with labor organizations in the East, created new ones shortly after coming to Michigan. By 1818 Detroit already had a Mechanics' Society. As towns sprang up along the roads that pierced the interior, other labor organizations were created. There is mention of a Workingmen's Society in Ypsilanti in 1830 and a Mechanics' Association in Marshall eight years later. Undoubtedly there were others that the local chroniclers failed to record.

The early unions differed from those of today, in that they were generally confined to a single locality. Moreover, a major purpose for organizing them was to provide mutual aid to members and their families in time of trouble. Private insurance company rates were high, and neither government nor employers offered benefits to workers. Thus the workers' own organizations provided the only form of accident or life insurance available.

Membership varied. Sometimes the master mechanics, and the journeymen in their shops, belonged to the same organization. The Marshall Mechanics' Association, for instance, was theoretically open to any mechanic or workingman in the township. The association even gave lowly apprentices some privileges. Other organizations were more restrictive. Some consisted solely of the master mechanics of a town and resembled employer associations rather than labor organizations. In addition to providing mutual aid, their members tried to hold the wage line on the journeymen who worked for them. The Detroit Mechanics' Society may have started out as this kind of an organization. But by 1825 all "practical Mechanics," masters and journeymen alike, could join.

Some of the early labor organizations also served an educational function. Most workers had received only a rudimentary education and it was difficult for them to educate themselves further. Public libraries were rare, even on the eastern seaboard. Books and magazines were expensive, and the individual worker normally could not afford to acquire a library of his own. As in many other areas in the nation, for men to have access to a collection of books, it was necessary to pool resources. The "diffusion of useful knowledge" was a primary objective of the Marshall Mechanics' Association, for example. Membership dues in that association could be paid in the form of books for its library. Saturday night debates on current topics also played an important role in the association's overall activities. The preamble of its constitution noted, "knowledge confers true dignity on human nature by exalting the mind to a sense of its powers."

The association attempted to improve its members' behavior as well as their minds. It stressed regular attendance at meetings and fulfillment of assigned duties. Fines were levied against those who were lax in such matters. The association also prescribed the correct conduct of those attending its meetings: "Members shall be seated and uncovered while the association is in session, and no smoking or prophane language, or illiberal personal remarks, shall be allowed, or any conversation held, which shall tend to interrupt the proceedings: Any person persisting in such conduct, after being called to order, shall be expelled from the meeting."

A few of the early labor organizations limited their membership exclusively to journeymen of one craft and focused on economic matters, a practice which became predominant among labor organization by the mid-nineteenth century. The earliest recorded example of this type in Michigan was an organization of journeymen carpenters in Detroit who banded together as a result of the depressed economic conditions that followed the Panic of 1837. Until the panic, Detroit had been the scene of wild land speculation and a frenzied building boom. The skilled craftsmen in the building trades had been able to command premium wages and a ten-hour day, in contrast to a normal working day of eleven or more hours. Once the speculative bubble burst, a depression set in, and the masters responded by cutting wages and increasing hours. The April 4, 1837, issue of a Detroit newspaper recorded the carpenters' reaction:

> Yesterday our streets were paraded by a large company of respectable looking journeymen carpenters, carrying standards bearing the pithy couplet
>
> "Ten hours a day
> And two dollars for pay."

Whether or not the carpenters achieved their goals is unrecorded. However, their organization was one of the few in Michigan to survive the depression years. Most labor unions were too weak to withstand downturns in the economic cycle.

Another early example of a local craft union was the Detroit Cordwainers Association, composed solely of journeymen shoemakers. In 1838, when their employers refused to grant them a higher piece rate, the union members called a strike and opened a cooperative shoestore of their own. The store did well, but its operators abandoned it the following year when their employers capitulated. As was characteristic of early unions, the cordwainers organization disbanded after its immediate ends were achieved. Thus if depression did not destroy the early labor organizations, their own immediate success did.

Printers were always among the first to organize along craft lines. In Michigan the Detroit Typographical Society was formed in April 1839, primarily as a means of pooling resources to aid members in distress. The organization included both journeymen and masters "among whom the very best feeling exists." The society was only two months old when the journeymen printers called a strike against one of the employer members for withholding wages. The employer, a newspaper owner, then tried to resign from the society, but the organization refused to accept his resignation and expelled him instead. One side effect of the strike was the publication of the state's first labor paper, *The Rat Gazette*. This was actually a strike bulletin, and probably no more than one issue ever appeared. *The Rat Gazette* was published in September 1839, four months after the strike began. In the interim, the struck newspaper succeeded in resuming publication on a nonunion basis. A major purpose in issuing the *Gazette* was to call attention to the "despicable race of vermin" who had agreed to work for the offending employer. It was quite common for printers, as for many other artisans, to move from job to job around the country, especially while they were still young and unmarried. The so-called tramp printer, for instance, was likely to turn up anywhere in search of work. Thus the *Gazette* listed each of the "rats" then working in Detroit by name and gave some sort of description of him—usually a rather insulting one. The Detroit society then circulated the *Gazette* to printers societies in other towns, so that they would have the rat list handy for the future. The issue also called attention to rats mentioned in previous communications among printers organizations and commented that Detroit printers hoped to enter into a regular correspondence with their brothers all over the country to be "rid of such sharks" once and for all.

The need for better communication among local societies became more acute as transportation facilities improved and the market for labor, as well as for product, expanded. In 1852, just over a decade after *The Rat Gazette* appeared, printers in the country created a national organization, the National Typographical Union, which became the International Typographical Union in 1869, with the addition of Canadian locals. The organization's function was to disseminate information on a regular basis and to establish firmer controls on the number and movement of members. The Detroit printers affiliated with the new union when it was formally organized. By then, employers were no longer involved.

The Civil War period spurred union activity everywhere.

Locally oriented organizations still predominated, but a number of national unions were also established. One of these, the Brotherhood of Locomotive Engineers (BLE), was founded in Michigan and became the first permanent railroad union in the country. A wartime atmosphere of full employment, high wages, and still higher prices had prompted the organization of the brotherhood. The specific catalyst was a change in the work rules, instituted by the Michigan Central Railroad late in 1862, which amounted to a wage cut for many of its employees. To vent their dissatisfaction, some of the Michigan Central's locomotive engineers met in Marshall—the "half-way house" on the Detroit–Chicago run—and decided to form a union. The organization was established in Detroit in May 1863 as the Brotherhood of the Footboard. It took its present name the following year at its first convention. By then the BLE had thirty-eight local divisions across the country. In 1883, twenty years after it was founded, the union had 234 locals and a membership of over 12,000

The BLE had two major functions: to foster the economic interests of the locomotive engineers and "to elevate their standing as such and their character as men." The emphasis on self-improvement was characteristic of many of the post-Civil War labor organizations. The stress on self-education was not merely a continuation of the earlier desire to "exalt the mind." As the Grand Chief Engineer told BLE conventioneers, they had to know more than "the business of simply running an engine" if they wanted to improve their working conditions and cope effectively with the problems posed by an increasingly complex industrial society.

By the end of the Civil War, railroads had spread throughout the country and had created a national mass market. This, in turn, hastened the introduction of machinery into manufacturing concerns, and, particularly in the North, the small shop steadily gave way to the sprawling factory, mill, and foundry. The ranks of the independent skilled artisans dwindled as machines came into use. The former craftsman became just another factory hand who worked at some assigned task for a low wage, eleven hours or more a day, six days a week. He competed for that job with the displaced farmer and the immigrant. Even in the best of times, he could not count on working steadily. Periodic unemployment was taken for granted—a natural consequence of "the inevitable law of supply and demand." A circular issued to call trade union leaders to a meeting pointed out that while, due to the introduction of the machine, "the power of production has doubled, consumption has not kept pace therewith, and as a consequence statistics show that on the average one-fourth of the labor of the country is idle at all times." During an economic recession, the effect on the urbanized industrial labor force was devastating.

Often wives and children entered the labor market to supplement the family income. Detroit women, for example, went to work in the local shoe factories and the garment industry. An 1866 study found that almost 2000 Detroit children were employed in shingle, match, and tobacco factories and in rag-picking establishments. Many of them were girls and some of them were no more than seven years old. As the gigantic corporation supplanted the small concern, individual contact between employer and employee ceased. Employers came to regard "labor" as a "commodity"—just another interchangeable part in the machine.

The average American industrial worker came to live an insecure, anonymous existence, and many of them doubtless agreed with a labor song of the time that

> The beasts that graze the hillside,
> The birds that wander free,
> In the life that God hath meted,
> Have a better lot than we.

The skilled workers who had not been replaced by the machine attempted to maintain their position by acting together through trade unions. Their efforts, however, met with fierce employer opposition, often with the backing of the courts and the government. The *Workingman's Advocate,* an influential labor paper, reflected the belief of many of the labor leaders of the time when it advised union members that they should "cherish" their organizations and "stick to them as the wrecked mariner clings to the last plank," but should also realize that "we can see no time in the future when this war between capital and 'trade unions' will have an end."

Moreover, unions represented only one element among American workers, the skilled, and this was not enough: "Let no trade believe that they can succeed alone, for the downfall of one class of our country's producers is an injury to all others; and if one body is compelled to succumb to the unjust demands of capital, all can rest assured that in turn they too will be overpowered." Trade unions were only stepping stones that aided those who were searching for "the agency that will give us permanent deliverance from our oppressors." Such "deliverance" required that all workers act together to educate themselves and one another in order, "first, to ascertain beyond a doubt why the workingmen of the country continue in a pover-

The first railroad YMCA was built in 1878 at Detroit. As they sprang up across the nation, the "Y's" became the railman's home away from home.

ty that is every year becoming more abject; and second, having ascertained the cause (s) prescribe and ENFORCE the remedy."

As the labor movement passed midcentury, it saw itself not striving merely to improve the worker's immediate economic position, but to make him a better man, living in a better world. These two goals—the one practical and short-run, the other idealistic and long-run—often came in conflict. Yet they dominated the history of organized labor in this country from the end of the Civil War to the closing years of the nineteenth century.

The Major Reform Movements

Reform efforts had achieved some importance as early as the 1830s and 1840s among workers along the eastern seaboard, the area affected earliest by urban concentration and the factory system. After the Civil War reform agitation continued and spread.

One issue was land reform. Its advocates urged that every man had a right to the land. They spoke of crowded housing conditions and high rents in the cities, while at the same time vast amounts of land lay unused throughout the country. They wanted the federal government to break up the large holdings that individual speculators, corporations, and railroads had acquired and to offer small farms to anyone who would actually settle on them. The immediate effect would be to draw off the unemployed from the towns and cities. This would ease the housing shortage, lower rents, and, moreover, create a scarcity of urban labor, which would force wages up.

Workingmen were also encouraged to form producer and consumer cooperatives. Adherents of the cooperative movement believed that this would have the immediate effect of lowering prices, since the middleman's profits would be eliminated. As the cooperative system spread and every man became a shareholder, the wage system would disappear altogether, they said.

Some labor leaders urged that an expansion of the money supply was the most important issue. Money was tight, and interest rates were high. The advocates of currency reform—usually called "Greenbackers" from the paper money ("greenbacks") issued by the federal government during the Civil

War—argued that until the worker had access to low-interest credit, he could not possibly take up farming or become part-owner of a cooperative. Greenbackers blamed the tight currency situation on the private banks of the country: the "money monopoly" that was parent to all other monopolies. They wanted the federal government, rather than the banks, to issue money, with the amount in circulation at any given time to be based on the needs of the country.

While some reformers wanted the government to take positive action in just one area (land redistribution, monetary policy), others believed that the worker would never receive his just share of the national wealth until the government played a stronger role in the American economy as a whole to check the unscrupulous who abused the free enterprise system. Some who held this view believed that the federal government could fulfill that function by taking over, or at least regulating, the country's transportation and communication facilities. Others went beyond that. They looked forward to the day when the country would be a socialist state and private property would be abolished altogether and all property, as well as all production and distribution, would be controlled by the government on behalf of all the people.

The reform cause that probably received the greatest support from American workers was the eight-hour movement. The adherents of a shorter workday pointed out that it would spread the available work among more people and thus relieve unemployment. Moreover, it would give the worker the leisure time he needed to educate himself. Interest in the eight-hour movement peaked in the United States during the 1860s. The eight-hour day became a common trade union bargaining demand and, moreover, numerous "eight-hour leagues" were formed to lobby for necessary legislation. Those leagues drew their membership not only from among workingmen but attracted countless other reform-minded citizens as well. At the time, the U.S. Supreme Court maintained the position that Congress had no power to legislate in such areas as maximum hours for any workers except those employed by the federal government. Thus the eight-hour advocates had to turn their major attention to the various state legislatures.

The labor reformers—whatever their particular cause—also counseled temperance. Workers should not waste their time in saloons or spend their money on "demon rum." They were urged instead to buy and read labor newspapers and hold discussions with their fellow workers on the current issues of the day. Because most of the advocated reforms also required legislative action, workers were urged to educate themselves to the issues, to know the candidates and what they stood for. Then they could act together, as informed citizens using their ballots to secure their rights.

The Reform Movements in Michigan—
the Trevellick Influence

Michigan labor was brought into the mainstream of the reform movements primarily because of Richard Trevellick, a British–born ship's carpenter who settled in Detroit in 1862. Trevellick had come to the United States in the late 1850s, after some years of work and travel in Australia, New Zealand, and along the west coast of South America. He originally settled in New Orleans, but came North after the outbreak of the Civil War. He was thirty-two when he moved to Detroit. Contemporaries described him as a man of "stout build" whose bushy dark beard half-covered a "fine ... but not peculiarly striking" face. He became noted as a well-informed and entertaining speaker—"The Eagle Orator of the West"—who could keep an audience spell-bound even in the dead of winter in an unheated theater as he alternated witticisms with statistical data. This was no mean feat, since his speeches usually ran two and a half hours!

After Trevellick moved to Michigan, he went to work for a Detroit dry dock company. Shortly thereafter, members of the Detroit local of one of the new national unions, the Ship Carpenters and Caulkers, elected him their president. Three years later, Trevellick became president of the national union and handled a Buffalo local's strike so shrewdly that the dry dock company fired and blacklisted him in retaliation. He was quickly reinstated, however, when his home local threatened to strike.

While Trevellick understood the need for the strike weapon,

he believed it should be used sparingly and only as a last resort. In common with many labor leaders of the time he preferred the boycott as a pressure device and also advocated "arbitration." (The term "arbitration" was then frequently used to mean simply the right of employee groups to sit down with employers to discuss their differences.) Trevellick hesitated to use the strike because union dues were low, and few organizations had the staying power to acquire an adequate strike fund. And the growing network of railroads, coupled with the increase in immigration to the country, made it increasingly easy for an employer to import outsiders rather than deal with his striking employees. Thus, in the end, walkouts were often far more damaging to the strikers than to their employers.

Trevellick was instrumental in establishing the Detroit Trades Assembly and became its first president. The assembly, a central labor body composed of representatives of most of the trade unions in the city, was similar to organizations which had been created in the east as early as 1827. Formed in 1864, the Detroit organization was the first of its kind in Michigan and soon numbered 5000 members, about 10 percent of the city's population. Although the assembly lasted only a few years, for a time it was a powerful force in Detroit. It served as spokesman for organized labor in economic matters and functioned effectively in city politics as well. Old-line politicians actively sought assembly support at election time, and, occasionally, workingmen themselves ran for city office, often successfully.

The same year in which Trevellick organized the assembly, he became involved in an effort to unite all such local central bodies into a national organization as a means of countering the emerging employers associations, formed to combat trade unionism. The national venture failed completely. The powerful eastern assemblies, jealous of their autonomy, were suspicious of the effort and refused to participate.

In his early days in Detroit, Trevellick's favorite reform cause was the eight-hour day. This was an interest of long-standing: he had been active in the movement during his years in Great Britain, Australia, and New Zealand. Largely through his efforts, Michigan had some 25 local eight-hour leagues by 1866. These in turn were affiliated with a statewide organization, the

Grand Eight-Hour League of Michigan, headed by Trevellick. With the active backing of the Detroit Trades Assembly, the eight-hour advocates successfully pressured the Detroit Common Council to enact an ordinance that covered most city government employees. But, despite all their efforts, they could not budge the state legislature.

Trevellick's activities on behalf of the shorter hours movement soon went beyond state borders, and he left his job with the dry docks company in order to devote full time to the cause. He shortly acquired a national reputation as one of the leading spokesmen for the eight-hour day. Trevellick also became heavily involved in the activities of a national organization, established in 1866, which initially had the eight-hour day as its major goal, though it subsequently shifted emphasis to currency reform. The National Labor Union's name reflected the fact that labor leaders from many places had been instrumental in founding it, and that it sought to foster the interests of American workingmen. It differed from the 1864 attempt to forge city central bodies into a national labor organization because it proposed to function primarily in the political arena, whereas the earlier body had been concerned with economic matters. The NLU also drew its members from a broader spectrum of American society and included representatives of farm organizations and middle-class reform societies, along with trade union leaders.

Within a few years internal dissension greatly weakened the NLU, and the Panic of 1873 destroyed it altogether. But initially it received wide support, and Trevellick worked tirelessly on its behalf. He helped establish a state affiliate to the NLU, the Michigan Labor Union, and served as its first president. For the Michigan body's first convention in December 1866, Trevellick drew up a political platform, which served as the basis for the national program adopted the following year.

The NLU chose Trevellick as its Washington lobbyist and, largely through his efforts, Congress granted federal employees the eight-hour day in 1868. In the end, the law proved a disappointment. It remained largely unenforced, and employees took a cut in pay as well as in hours in places where it was put into practice. Trevellick and others continued to badger Congress and the President to apply the law uniformly and fairly, but with indifferent success.

The eight-hour legislation enacted in a few of the states during the 1860s proved even more discouraging. It normally included an escape clause which stipulated that eight hours constituted a legal day's work only in the absence of a written contract between employer and employee to the contrary. Where such a document existed, the law did not apply. In consequence, immediately after such legislation was passed, printing firms did a brisk business with employers requesting mass-produced contract forms, and the legislation was ineffective thereafter.

Such meager results led many to conclude that it was useless to work within the existing political framework to obtain favorable labor legislation. To some, Trevellick among them, the

Richard Trevellick

logical next step was independent political action. As president of the NLU (from 1869 to 1872), Trevellick was among those who attempted to turn the organization into a new political party, the National Labor Reform Party. When that proved a failure, he helped to launch another new party, the Greenback-Labor Party, and became a prominent figure in it. Trevellick had become discouraged with efforts to shorten the working day and had turned to currency reform: "let the money question be the question . . . ," he said. "The masses can never have the rights that belong to them as long as the present thieving money system remains in force." He was a tireless organizer for the party, and once while stumping for it, he wrote a friend that he "spoke seventeen times, organized sixteen Greenback Clubs, smashed up a buggy and got pitched in the mud—all in twelve days. Who can beat that?" Throughout, Trevellick maintained an all-encompassing concern for the American worker. He was one of the few who attempted to organize western agricultural workers. He pleaded incessantly with trade union groups to help the women in the garment industry obtain better wages and led a successful boycott against a Detroit clothier to that end. He was also one of the first to show concern for black workers.

Not all labor leaders agreed with Trevellick's emphasis on politics, particularly if this meant independent political action. The "pure and simple" trade unionists argued that since organized labor represented a minority of the voters, it was useless to exert energy on independent politicking. Some thought that any time spent on politics was a waste of time—such effort could be better spent at the bargaining table. Argument over political activity caused the Detroit Trades Assembly to disband and was a major cause for the dissension within the NLU. Those who disagreed with Trevellick were primarily skilled workers, men who usually had the necessary economic power to make bargaining work. Trevellick's view had greater appeal to those who lacked bargainable skills and who viewed the political road as the only one open.

Nonetheless, even the most ardent advocates of "pure and simple" trade unionism often came to agree with Trevellick in time of economic turmoil when collective bargaining efforts were relatively fruitless. During the post-Civil War recession, they flocked to the NLU, fully aware that it was politically oriented. It was only when prosperity returned that they became critical of the organization's emphasis upon political action and withdrew. When they deserted the NLU the skilled men also criticized its devotion to currency reform. Yet in the depression years that followed the Panic of 1873 they changed their minds: "Our mechanics and laboring men are sorely feeling the hard times and . . . commenced to think that there is something wrong and rotten in the financial policy of the government, which policy is making the rich richer and the poor poorer. This policy can only be changed by legislation, which would put labor on an equality with aggregated capital." "Politics," they said, "is bread."

Thus even the "elites" in the labor movement had no permanent answer to the question whether labor should follow a political or an economic path.

The Knights of Labor

In the late 1870s, while Trevellick was still stumping for the greenbackers, a new labor organization came into prominence which attempted to settle the question of labor's proper role by engaging in both political and economic activity: the Noble and Holy Order of the Knights of Labor. The order was established in 1869 by nine Philadelphia garment cutters. At first it was no different from any other local craft union except that it insisted upon secrecy. Within a year, however, the garment cutters were initiating "sojourners," workers in other trades who were expected to "swarm" from the parent organization and form local unions, called "assemblies," of their own. Until 1874 the organization remained confined to the Philadelphia area. But by then, the depression of 1873-79 had caused the collapse of many earlier labor organizations, and their members began turning to the order. The Knights' emphasis upon secrecy gave the organization a protective covering in the face of employer hostility that permitted it to grow steadily.

Initially, except for the temporary "sojourners," the local assemblies were always composed solely of workers in a single trade. As the order grew and reached out to the less industrialized regions, catch-all units, called "mixed assemblies," became more common. Where a number of local assemblies existed in an area, they often grouped themselves into district assemblies. In 1878 the Knights held their first national convention, or General Assembly, and created the office of Grand Master Workman and other national posts.

Even after the Knights developed a national framework, it continued as a secret society. In time, however, its secrecy proved to be more of a liability than an asset. The order grew too large to remain hidden, and rumors that exaggerated its size and misstated its purposes caused widespread public alarm. Consequently, at the 1881 General Assembly, held in Detroit, the Knights officially came out in the open. At this convention the order also shed certain rituals of a quasi-religious nature that were causing criticism, particularly from the Catholic Church. Thereafter, for example, the order no longer described itself as either "noble" or "holy."

The Knights of Labor grew steadily after that. By 1882 the organization had over 42,000 members. At its peak in 1886, there were over 700,000 Knights of Labor in the country enrolled in nearly 6000 local units. Membership in the Knights of Labor was not limited to skilled artisans. Nor did sex, race, creed, or nationality constitute a barrier. The Knights' motto, "an injury to one is the concern of all," reflected the organization's governing principle of labor solidarity—the belief in "the great brotherhood of toil." Three quarters of the members of each local were required to be wage earners, but the organization welcomed "all branches of honorable toil." The "drones" in society—doctors, lawyers, bankers, stockbrokers—were not acceptable. Nor were professional gamblers allowed or persons engaged in the sale of alcoholic beverages. Doctors were taken off the prohibited list in 1884. Someone also suggested facetiously that lawyers ought to be allowed in, since they were so much like carpenters: They "can file a bill, split a hair, chop logic, dovetail an argument, . . . get up a case, frame an indictment, . . . nail a witness, . . . bore a court, [and] chisel a client."

The Knights of Labor officially opposed strikes and urged "arbitration" instead. The order used the boycott extensively and developed the technique into an extremely effective weapon. Through its national newspaper, the *Journal of United Labor,* as well as other local labor papers, the organization gave wide publicity to products that it had under boycott. Readers were urged not to buy, haul, work with, or service boycotted products. The use of the boycott was widened to include merchants and jobbers who sold such articles. Conversely, the Knights gave extensive favorable publicity to articles that bore the union label.

The Knights' program emphasized reforms: the establishment of consumer and producer cooooperatives, changes in land and currency policies, shorter hours, and temperance. It also stressed education and political awareness. It was only natural that Richard Trevellick soon joined the Knights, given their reform-tinged program and emphasis upon labor solidarity. He became one of its most indefatigable and successful organizers and remained with the order for the rest of his life.

A Michigan Knight—Joseph Labadie

Trevellick was not the first Michigan labor leader to join the Knights. He was still immersed in greenbackism when Joseph Labadie, a man some twenty years his junior, was already busy organizing the first local assembly in the state.

Labadie was born in Paw Paw, Michigan, in the late 1840s, but as a child and as a young "tramp" printer he was gone from his home state much of the time until 1872, when he settled in Detroit. Labadie was a big man, always carefully groomed, with a luxuriant mop of black hair that swept back from his forehead in a stylish pompadour. He also sported a neatly clipped goatee and sweeping handlebar moustache. Because of his size and the fact that on his mother's side he was descended from a Potawatomi chief, his friends called him "the Big Injun." He was a good-natured, friendly man. He read widely, was well informed, and enjoyed nothing more than a good argument on topics of current interest. He was a gentle man, but the workers' plight nearly drove him to violence: "to know and to *experience* the feelings of being out of work through no fault of your own," he wrote, "with a family to support and no money nor credit, . . . the abuse and insults heaped upon workers by brutal employers and bosses . . . I often *feel* as though the just punishment for the class of people who abuse the power they have, as employers and landlords and monopolists do generally, is total annihilation by any and every means at our command."

Like Trevellick, Labadie outspokenly advocated reform. The same year that he organized the Knights' first Michigan assembly he was also deeply involved in the currency reform cause and ran an unsuccessful race as mayor of Detroit on the Greenback ticket. However, he was unlike Trevellick and other older labor reformers in some respects. In much of their program the older men were basically trying to turn back the clock to the days of the artisan-farmer. When they emphasized cooperatives, land reform, and the like, they were aiming to make it easier for the worker to be self-employed—to return to the land or to open up a small shop. Labadie and other younger labor leaders were less nostalgic. Industrialism and urbanism were, to them, permanent features on the American scene. It was useless to try to go back to a simpler time. The large class of landless wage earners were a part of a system that could not be wished away; it was important to have a decent life within it. Thus while Labadie was a firm adherent of currency reform, his reasons for believing in it had little to do with a desire to return to "the good old days." He felt that a larger volume of currency would increase prices of manufactured goods. As prices went up, manufacturers would be encouraged to produce more and, in doing so, would add to their work force. In turn, the newly employed would be able to increase their consumption. Their demands would create a need for more production, which would require an even larger work force. In the end, all factories would be humming, and everyone would be employed.

While Labadie accepted industrialism, he did not believe in the free enterprise system. To him, capitalism was "the one thing in the world that stands between the useful worker and the full results of his efforts. This is why it should be abolished." He was one of the first in Michigan to become interested in socialism, because he believed that the state would be a more equitable employer than the private corporation. For a time, he was an active member of the Socialist Labor Party, although by the mid-1880s he had abandoned what he termed his "Marxmanship," because he concluded that it merely substituted one overly powerful authority for another.

In the 1870s, however, Labadie was still attracted to what he later called the "fever of governmentalism." While his goals for the American worker might not have been precisely the same as those envisioned by the older leaders of the Knights, Labadie found the order's overall program attractive, and he worked very diligently to interest Michigan workers in it.

He organized Michigan's first local assembly in Detroit in 1878 while the Knights of Labor was still a secret society. Accordingly, the local organization bore the purposely misleading title of "The Washington Literary Society." Labadie was its original master workman. He also was appointed the order's first organizer in Michigan.

For a few years his efforts produced meager results. Only two Michigan local assemblies were represented at the 1881 General Assembly in Detroit: the one he had founded in Detroit and a Jackson coalminers* group. Thereafter, however, interest increased and he could report that "I organized several assemblies in Detroit, and in a comparatively short time we spread out over the State and honeycombed it with assemblies composed of mechanics, farmers, laborers, small storekeepers, and all classes except lawyers, who were barred from membership."

By July 1885 there were six district assemblies, 160 locals, and 7,603 Knights of Labor in Michigan. It is estimated that the following year, when membership reached its peak, there were some 25,000 members of the order in the state. By then, Labadie had also formally organized a state assembly. Because of the order's all-inclusive membership policy, only a rough estimate can be made of what the 1886 figure might mean in terms of organization among nonagricultural wage earners in Michigan. At most, Knights and trade unions together probably could not have drawn more than 10 percent of that group in 1886. While that figure does not seem very impressive, it still rep-

---

* Although most present-day Michiganders are unaware that there are substantial low-grade coal deposits in their state, the fact is that coal was mined extensively in Michigan well into the twentieth century. In the 1880s, three producing mines existed in Jackson and one in Shiawassee. The Jackson mines employed over 250 coalminers.

resented quite an achievement for the time and would not be duplicated again until World War I. Even today, less than 30 percent of the nonagricultural labor force is organized.

The 1880s saw a marked increase in the use of the strike in the country by the Knights, the traditional trade unions, and hitherto unorganized workers. In Michigan from 1881 through 1886 there were 358 recorded walkouts, and there were probably others as well that were either too short or too unimportant to receive official notice. The Knights leadership became involved in many of them, whether or not they were called by local affiliates.

Despite the order's emphasis on cooperatives, only a few were actually established in Michigan: a coal and woodyard in Grand Rapids, a store in Bay City, a company that made road carts and buckboards in Kalamazoo, a Battle Creek building material and coal outlet, and a boot and shoe store in Detroit. In common with such efforts elsewhere, the Michigan cooperatives eventually failed. Some were mismanaged from the start; others that were initially successful expanded too rapidly and were unable to obtain credit when overextension caught up with them.

The order was extremely active in politics everywhere. Usually its members were able to influence one of the established political parties and work with it to nominate candidates pledged to support the Knights' program. In a few areas, members of the order took independent action. Michigan Knights were particularly successful in politics and often were able to get their own members nominated by either or both major political parties. There were three Knights in the 1883 state legislature and eighteen at the next session in 1885. Two years later there were thirty-eight, not including other sympathizers. There were many local election victories as well, particularly in the state's lumbering areas where the Knights were especially numerous.

In the long run, such successes came to very little. In 1883 the legislature did pass an act creating a state Bureau of Labor and Industrial Statistics. Some child labor and safety legislation was also subsequently enacted. But most bills introduced by Knights or their sympathizers either failed to pass or were meaningless by the time they were enacted, because they were so watered down. Moreover, the candidates themselves proved a disappointment once in office. After the election, promises were easily forgotten. In 1884, at the height of the enthusiasm for political action, an influential Detroit labor paper urged its readers to "punish your enemies first, then reward your friends." As time passed, members of the order wondered how to tell them apart.

Disillusionment with the meager results of these political efforts was one factor in the decline of the Knights of Labor. There were others. Some members disliked the reform emphasis. Others thought the leaders were inept and disliked their conservative approach to collective bargaining and strike action. The temperance issue provided an additional bone of contention. To many immigrant workers, accustomed to their glass of beer or cup of wine, the emphasis on abstinence was incomprehensible. But the cultural difference was not the only factor. As a union man explained:

> Most of our active workers opposed the saloon when they were young members of the organization, but experience with the work of the union was responsible for a radical change in their views. It is difficult to secure suitable meeting places not connected with saloons in some way. Many unions meet in halls in the rear of saloons, while others meet over saloons. In many instances no rent is charged, and small organizations are encouraged to battle against adverse conditions because of their minimum expenses. ... [Moreover] this institution is looked upon by the vast majority of workingmen as their club. When out of employment the workingman can get a free lunch and meet a congenial soul to cheer him in the saloon when there is nothing but discouragement for him elsewhere.

Perhaps the most important factor in the decline of the Knights was the growing rivalry between the Knights and the national trade unions. Until the mid-1880s the two groups often worked together. In 1884, for example, the district assemblies in Michigan and the Detroit Council of Trades and Labor Unions (a city central body) jointly sponsored a drive to raise funds to build a home for Richard Trevellick. Labadie, incidentally, served as treasurer of that fund. But such cooperation did not last. Friction increased after 1885 when the nation began to recover from an economic slump; and the Knights and trade unions expanded rapidly. Rivalry was most evident between local Knights assemblies composed solely of workers from a particular craft and trade union locals whose members were of the same craft. The trade union organizer found that if he tried to enter a locality where a single-craft Knights assembly existed, he either had to leave the town to its jurisdiction or prepare to battle it out. Where no such assembly existed, he set up a local union which drew off skilled men from the mixed assembly and incurred the wrath of the rest.

In this charged atmosphere some of the stronger national trade unions banded together in 1886 to form a new labor organization, the American Federation of Labor (AFL). It aimed to coordinate the efforts of the individual trade unions in defeating the Knights. Within a few years the AFL was victorious, and by the end of the nineteenth century the "great brotherhood of toil" was moribund.

In Michigan the last Detroit local assembly of the Knights ceased to function in 1892. The state assembly lingered on for a few more years but drew its membership almost solely from the rural districts.

Three years earlier, in 1889, a state affiliate of the AFL, the Michigan Federation of Labor (MFL), had already been established. At its first convention the presiding officer explained that the MFL had been formed because "mixed labor organizations have proven to be a sad failure." He assured his listeners that the new body would function only as a lobbying and educational vehicle, and that the constituent unions would be autonomous in the economic realm: "A horse-shoer on a labor committee would be as improper a person for negotiations on a printers' strike as would be the devil as an appraiser of the influence of holy mass on an expired soul."

Joseph Labadie played a major role in founding the MFL and served as its first president. He had left the Knights two years earlier. Labadie's interest in the AFL paralleled his new enthusiasm in another area. He, like the leading figures in the

Federation, was disillusioned with the results of organized labor's earlier political efforts. But unlike them, he did not believe that economic activity and the short-run gains made at the bargaining table would solve labor's problems permanently. Instead, Labadie embraced anarchism. This, he now held, was the final solution.

Labadie was a philosophical anarchist, a brand of anarchism that was eminently peaceful and laid strong stress on individual freedom. It grew out of the belief that man is basically good but is fettered and corrupted by authoritarian institutions. No longer did Labadie believe that a stronger government would benefit the workingman. Government, he now said, was "the means by which the state crushes out personal freedom, monopolizes the land, the currency, the machinery for the benefit of the privileged class and makes involuntary poverty a necessary

Joseph Labadie

consequence." His mistrust of the government reached a point where he was ready to do away with the public school system, which, to Labadie, was just "an excuse to bolster up our bad social and industrial conditions."

Despite Labadie's distaste for institutions, he continued to favor trade unions as he always had. During his years as a Knight and political reformer, Labadie never had abandoned his association with trade unions. He remained an active member. of the International Typographical Union during those years and was a prime mover in creating, in 1880, a forerunner of the Metropolitan Detroit AFL-CIO, the Detroit Council of Trades and Labor Unions. He also acted as the council's first president. After he embraced anarchism Labadie still maintained, "It is no theory, but a plain fact, that better wages and better conditions are granted members of the unions than to non-members," But unions were only a temporary expedient. As Labadie saw it, "Correct knowledge of true social laws must first become general, so much so as to mold public opinion to the fact that in the long run it is best to do right." When everyone was convinced of that, there would be no need for associations of any kind. And Labadie was sure that eventually "evolution will produce the desired end."

Labadie was a very popular figure in Michigan labor circles. The "gentle anarchist," as he was often called, was much in demand on the banquet circuit and as featured speaker at union meetings. Labadie also had a far-flung correspondence. He was said to know more people in more places than any man in Michigan. He also contributed innumerable articles to labor newspapers throughout the country and, for a time, wrote a regular column, "Cranky Notions," for a Detroit labor paper. Fortunately for later generations, Labadie was a "pack-rat." He collected everything—newspapers, books, pamphlets, banquet programs, leaflets, letters, photographs—and saved it all. In 1911 he sold the material he had accumulated to the University of Michigan library. The Labadie Collection, now expanded through gifts and purchases, serves as a major source for what is known about Michigan labor history in the last half of the nineteenth century.

2

"TEN HOURS OR NO SAWDUST"

It is difficult now to realize that the Saginaw Valley was once a major lumbering area in the United States. The huge stands of virgin white pine have long since vanished, and with them the colorful lumberjacks who sang about their days in the Michigan woods:

> The grub the dogs would laugh at
> Our beds were on the snow
> God send us to no worse than hell
> Or Michigan-I-O.

Lumbering in the United States had initially been centered in the Northeast: Maine, New York, and Pennsylvania. As the supply of trees dwindled, new sources were sought. The Saginaw Valley's seemingly endless supply of pine coupled with easy water transport to eastern markets assured early exploitation. The first shipment from the Valley reached Albany in 1847. Less than forty years later over a billion feet of lumber left the area every year, and both banks of the Saginaw River were dotted with mills from the Saginaws* to Bay City.

The trees were felled in the winter when it was easy to skid logs over the frozen ground and to pile them up in log ponds or along the shores of the icy Saginaw and its tributaries. In the spring, as the ponds and rivers thawed and the woods became boggy, men and logs moved downriver to the mills where the winter's haul was processed for sale.

The Valley, like much of Michigan's lower peninsula, sits on an ancient ocean bed. About a decade after lumbering had begun there on a commercial basis, salt production was undertaken as well. Initially, salt establishments and lumber companies had been separately owned and operated, although the salt producers always purchased the readily available lumber scrap to produce barrels and to stoke the fires that were necessary to evaporate the brine. It was soon clear, however, that salt production alone was not sufficiently profitable. By 1866 lumber companies had taken over the operation of the salt blocks. The integration of the two industries proved financially sound, although salt production always remained a by-product of the more profitable lumber industry. Nonetheless, that "sideline" was producing three million barrels of salt a year by the 1880s.

Some of the men who worked in the sawmills and salt blocks in summer also logged in winter, although this was by no means always true. Fewer hands were needed in the woods. In addition, in each type of work, milling or logging, there was some fluctuation in employment within the working season. Work in the woods peaked in January and February. In the mills, June through August were the months of highest employment. Salt production continued about two and a half months after the sawmills had closed for the season, until the lumber scrap ran out. This afforded work for some who could not find jobs in the lumber camps. Even so, few men could count on year-round employment.

There were a number of small farming communities in the Valley before large-scale lumbering was begun. Nevertheless, as was true whenever such operations moved into a new area, the

---

* East Saginaw and Saginaw City were separate municipalities until 1889, when they were combined to form the present-day city of Saginaw.

companies were forced to go into the housing business if they were to attract labor. In the lumber camps very simple barracks-like structures served the purpose. Around the mills the companies constructed boarding houses for single men, which were either rented or sold outright to persons interested in running them. Even if the companies no longer owned the buildings, the wages they paid governed what the landlords could charge. Small cottages were also built and rented to the married men and their families. Rents ranged from $6 to $10 a month depending upon the size of the cottage. While this may seem astonishingly low rent in present-day terms, for the time it was not. In fact, a perusal of the "want ads" section in a contemporary Detroit newspaper would indicate that the cottages were no bargain at all. Beyond this, while millowners cut back wages when lumber prices went down, their rental charges remained

Sorting logs on the river in the Saginaw Valley, scene of the strike against millowners in 1885

stable from one year to the next. With little alternate housing available in the Valley, the millhands had no choice but to stay where they were and pay the price.

The companies also became merchants while organizing their communities, and the "company store" was a feature common to most milltowns. During the economic depression of the 1870s, the companies in the Valley issued "store orders" on payday instead of cash. By the 1880s this was no longer a general practice, but employees still tended to trade at those stores primarily because they were able to charge what they needed. Many companies paid only once a month and, in addition, often held back a portion of the season's wages until the final pay period, as a means of holding the employee to his job. Wages were low, and in order to get by until payday the employee was almost forced to trade at the company store.

Workers expressed some dissatisfaction with the stores' prices and also complained that the rents were too high. The high costs were particularly burdensome in 1885 because almost all of the mills had cut wage rates by 10 percent to 20 percent from those paid the previous season. The millowners explained that they could not continue to pay the old rates because business was slow. The men would have to take a pay cut. One employer reported that, in his mill, wages dropped from $1.98 to $1.72 a day between 1884 and 1885. Overall, men working in the mills averaged $1.77 a day in 1885 while those in and around the salt blocks averaged $1.73. Boys under sixteen—and there were almost 600 of them on company payrolls—got $.93 a day in the mills and $.85 at the salt blocks.

Even with the pay cut, some mills did not open for the season, and employment was down. Labor papers warned those seeking jobs in the lumber industry that there was nothing for them in the Saginaw Valley. As the Detroit *Labor Leaf* put it, "the Saginaw Valley is a good place to stay away from."

It was in this setting that the most important strike in nineteenth century Michigan history took place. The walkout began right after the July 4 weekend, in 1885, and, for a time, lumber and salt production were virtually at a standstill throughout the Valley.

What came to be called the Great Strike in the Valley did not center on the wage issue, housing, or the prices at the company stores. In the early days of the strike, the strikers did ask that, in the future, wages be paid every two weeks, but that issue faded quickly as the strike wore on. The basic purpose of the strike was to achieve a ten-hour day with no further cut in daily wages. At the time, workers put in from eleven to eleven and a half hours a day, six days a week. The work was physically exhausting, especially during the heat of the summer, and left little time or energy for anything else. Moreover, it was danger-ous—safety features were few, and mishaps mounted as the day dragged on.

Over a decade earlier, in 1872, the men in the Valley also struck for a ten-hour day. The earlier strike had been unorga-nized, short-lived, and unsuccessful. However, by July 1885 the goal seemed more attainable. Ten hours and even less were becoming a standard day's work in much of the country. Be-yond this, in early June the Michigan legislature had passed a law that limited a day's work to ten hours in most undertakings, including sawmills and salt blocks. The Valley newspapers had reported its passage, although they had failed to say that the law did not take effect until September 20. Consequently, some of the men thought that it became a law on July 1.

Although this misconception is often cited as a major reason for the strike, it may be that too much emphasis has been placed on that. Sentiment for shorter hours had been growing long before the bill was signed into law and this probably would have exploded into a strike in any event.

At the beginning of the milling season some of the millown-ers and their employees had discussed the shorter work day; but the employers would grant the concession only if it were cou-pled with an even greater wage reduction. The workers had refused. There had apparently been some talk of a strike during the spring, for when the author of the ten-hour bill spoke to workmen's meetings in the Valley, he specifically stated that "a fair discussion of the matter [of the shorter work day] be-tween employers and employees would result in its being ad-justed without a strike." The bill's author, Thomas Barry, had been elected to the state legislature from Saginaw County on the Democratic-Greenback ticket and was an ardent supporter of the workingman. He had sponsored a number of prolabor bills during the year, but only his ten-hour bill met with any success at all. Even in this, Barry's victory was less than complete, because when the bill was finally signed into law, it contained an escape clause typical of such legislation at the time. If a written contract between employer and employee existed agreeing to longer hours, the law was inapplicable.

Barry was also an organizer for the Knights of Labor and a member of that organization's general executive board. Interest in the Knights was very strong in the Valley, and there were numerous local assemblies. These, for the most part, were attached to one of two district assemblies, one in East Saginaw and the other in Bay City, although a few local assemblies were directly affiliated with the General Assembly. Following the pattern of other less industrialized regions of the country, the composition of the local assemblies in the Valley varied considerably. A few were organized by trade (carpenters and woodworkers, ironworkers, longshoremen); others by nationality (French Canadian, German, Polish). Blacks were in one local assembly, women in another. Still others were simply labeled "mixed."

The ten-hour issue had been the topic of at least one local's meeting and probably came up at others. The following circular, addressed to the millowners of Saginaw City and South Saginaw, may have been the product of one of these gatherings or, perhaps, the result of one of Barry's speeches:

Saginaw City, May 6, 1885

Dear Sir:

At a joint meeting of the labor organizations of Saginaw City and South Saginaw, a committee of seven was appointed to confer with a like committee of mill owners in regard to Hours to be worked in the mills. We believe that the hours of labor in the mills should be reduced to 10 per day. We further believe that it will be better for mill owners, as well as to the workingmen; and for this reason we wish to meet the owners of mills on fair and impartial footing, and endeavour to come to a satisfactory understanding. We therefore request, that the mill owners of Saginaw City and

South Saginaw meet and appoint a committee of seven to confer with us. Please name the place of meeting, and at any time within two weeks from the date of this request. Any place you please to name in Saginaw City for the meeting of the Committee will satisfy us.

The K. of L. Hall, in Beach & Andrew Block, Court Street, can be had free of charge, on any afternoon.

> Yours Respectfully,
> ABBOT E. LAWRENCE
> Chairman, Workingmen's Committee

Lawrence was a member of the Knights of Labor and also chief of police in Saginaw City. No information has turned up as to the other members of the "workingmen's committee," other than that they, too, were Knights of Labor.

Later, after the strike began, and the head of Michigan's Bureau of Labor and Industrial Statistics, the state commissioner of labor, came to the Valley to investigate the conflict, he was told that similar circulars had been sent to all of the employers, although his investigator could not locate any others. Indeed, the investigator had to dig hard to turn up the one quoted above. The millowners denied knowledge of them. One Saginaw City man admitted that "he thought that in the spring he heard some of his men talking about the matter," but also added that "he never heard it spoken of among the mill owners." The closest thing to an admission came from another millowner, who was also the mayor of East Saginaw. When questioned by a Detroit newspaperman, he said, "The nearest approach to anything of the sort was the request published in our home newspapers, with the signature of Chief of Police Lawrence of Saginaw City and other Knights of Labor that the mill owners should meet them to settle on a scale. We were not notified individually, so of course we paid no attention to it."

Whatever the merits of the denials, the workers believed that their employers had all received a notice, and at least one reporter thought that the owners' refusal to meet with the committee was a key factor in precipitating the strike. By June it was generally rumored that something was going to happen to force the issue right after the July Fourth weekend.

Agitation initially centered in the Bay City area, where a member of the Knights, D. C. Blinn, was in contact with the labor community through his newspaper, the *Labor Vindicator.* Blinn's appeal for concerted action must have been particularly attractive to the Polish community. The "Polanders," as they were called, had been brought into the Valley two years earlier as a source of cheap labor, and they generally held the lowest paying jobs and worked the longest hours. Shortly before the strike they requested and received a charter from the Knights to form their own local assembly. In the early stages of the strike the Bay City Polanders were its backbone.

The strike itself began on Monday, July 6. One mill, close to Bay City, was closed that morning for repairs, and the men who had come to work there were heading home. The millowner described what happened next: "One man, John Beaskey, took a bandana handkerchief from another man's pocket, fastened it to a stick, and, as they were near McEwen's mill, waved it in the air and shouted, 'Hurrah for ten hours.' McEwen's mill was not running, some of the men not having got over the 'Fourth,' and the others were around the mill. The shouting of the man started them going, and the strike began." The men then went to another mill that was in operation. They were met there by the Bay County sheriff and told to move on, which they did. The strikers were soon joined by men who had been unable to find work during the season. While the millowners and others roundly denounced these "idlers" for taking part in the strike and stirring up trouble, the unemployed actually had a big stake in its success. One argument commonly made in favor of the ten-hour day was that it would provide work for more people.

Early in the day the strikers contacted Blinn, who joined with them and took over leadership of the strike. They moved from mill to mill, stood outside each one, and shouted at those working there to come out and join them. Although their success that day and the next was not overwhelming and many of the mills kept running, the movement kept gaining momentum.

Wednesday morning, July 8, the band of strikers was more successful. The first three mills approached shut down; each shut-down added to the ranks. As the men neared the fourth mill the crowd numbered an estimated 800. During much of this time, as during the first two days of the strike, the Bay County sheriff and some of his men accompanied them. However, as long as the group was orderly and a millowner did not specifically order the sheriff to keep the strikers away, he and his men made no attempt to interfere. If a millowner did protest, the sheriff simply asked the men to move on.

The sheriff described what happened that morning at the fourth mill:

> The men were getting more boisterous and noisy and were determined to stop the mill. They had clubs and were shouting; men went into the mill; they were ordered out, and went. Loaded carts attempted to come out, and the crowd commenced throwing clubs at the horses and drivers. I had six deputies and six policemen and endeavored to stop them. The men had clubs, and both myself and my officers were hit. We arrested two of the leaders and I was hit with a slab. I sent them to the station. A third man was arrested at the Third Street bridge for striking a policeman, and he was sent to the station. We in the end drove them off. . . .
>
> I went to the lockup to see the men who were arrested. Chief of Police Murphy had struck one of the men after their arrest, and it was at once reported that he had killed him, and great excitement was created and a large crowd gathered. I ordered them to go away, and told them the man was not hurt and that they should be dealt with fairly. Many went away but still the crowd increased, many coming through curiosity. I went to the prosecuting attorney to advise an immediate hearing for these men to allay the excitement. The crowd wanted the men bailed at once. . . .
>
> On going back, I learned that the mayor, George H. Shearer, was going to release the men. I found him at the lockup ready to let the men go. I forbade him doing so, and I said I had rather see the lockup torn down than do it. But the mayor was . . . bound to let the men go. . . . This action of the mayor kicked the pluck all out of the police.

The arrests and subsequent releases were considered a turning point in the strike. Some believed that interest in the strike snowballed because of the way the police chief mistreated the arrested striker. Others blamed what they believed to be the mayor's lack of backbone. As one man put it, "when our mayor released the men who had been arrested ... he, in effect, told the crowd that a mistake had been made in arresting the men, or that the crowd could run things to suit themselves."

Up to this point, strike activity was confined to the Bay City area, and even there mills and salt blocks had still been operating that morning; although by afternoon none were. Around the Saginaws there was then no strike activity at all, and all establishments were running at full crew. Perhaps the men were waiting to see what would happen downriver.

On Thursday, July 9, the day after the arrests, Thomas Barry came to Bay City. He was then in the midst of a "dockwollopers" strike in East Saginaw, and one reason that he and some fifty of the striking dockhands came downriver was to encourage the Bay City longshoremen to join them. He also invited the Bay City millhands to come to the Saginaws the following day and spread the strike for the ten-hour day there.

The following morning an estimated 500 men piled into barges and tugs at Bay City and headed upriver. Some carried banners showing their slogan: "Ten hours or no sawdust." They were met at the East Saginaw docks by Barry, his striking dockwollopers, and a band. The combined force was estimated at between 1000 and 1200.

The group spent the afternoon closing down one mill after another. By the end of the day very few mills were still running. Overall, there was very little violence, although Barry was at times hard-pressed to keep the sizable crowd under control. In some mills the workers resisted the call to shut down and were carried out bodily. In another, Barry rescued a foreman from a likely severe clubbing. At no time did the Saginaw County sheriff or his men interfere in any way.

That evening, the Bay City men went home, and the Saginaw contingent shut down the rest of the mills in their area the following day. When they were done, they had shut down nearly ninety mills and over fifty salt blocks in the Saginaw Valley, and some 6000 people were idle.

During the morning, as the men were closing the rest of the Saginaw mills, trouble broke out when some of the strikers returned to a mill to put out the evaporation fires under its salt blocks. The millowner wrested the hose they were using from the men and turned it on them. The strikers rushed him. Two maintenance men, who had remained on the job, came to their employer's defense, and the strikers attacked them as well, injuring all three. Barry rushed to their defense, and one later testified that Barry had saved his life.

The same morning, in Bay City, a three-man committee representing the strikers met with a committee of area millowners and presented their demands: ten hours with no reduction in wages, payday every two weeks, and no blacklisting when the

Thomas Barry

strike was over. That afternoon they received their answer; the millowners "did not propose to have outsiders dictate to them in regard to the operation of their mills." They "didn't mean to oppress the men," but they had always been able to settle grievances amicably with their employees in the past, and this is what they proposed to do in the future. They would meet with no one else.

At a rally following the committee meetings, Blinn described what had happened. In a fiery speech he criticized the millowners for their unwillingness to meet the demands and virtually called for a general strike in retaliation: stablemen should quit and let the millmen feed their own horses; hired girls should leave and let the millowners' wives do their own cooking "Let all persons who labor quit, and see how they can get along without labor."

Blinn also stated that the strike would now receive help from "a greater power than it has had." This was taken to mean that the Knights of Labor would step in officially. Prominent Knights in the city quickly denied this and severely criticized Blinn's volatile speech. As the Bay County sheriff later put it, the Bay City Knights "shut down on Blinn" that evening. From then on, Thomas Barry, who had previously confined his efforts primarily to the Saginaws, was in charge of the Great Strike in the whole Valley.

The Bay City Knights actually did become involved the following day, Sunday. That afternoon, the Bay City area district assembly appointed a committee to confer with employer representatives, and on Monday a three-hour meeting took place. The result was a Knights offer to mediate the dispute. In the end, nothing came of this proposal. The millowners reiterated their flat refusal to deal with anyone other than their own employees.

The millowners were far from idle during the first days of the strike. They prodded the local authorities to take whatever action was necessary to protect their property and threatened to hold the cities liable for damages. Some in the Saginaw area, outside city jurisdiction, told county authorities that they would start up again the following Monday, and if interference were permitted, they would sue the county at the rate of $500 a day.

Initially, these threats met with indifferent success. After the Bay City mayor reported the owners' warnings to his common council, a resolution was put before that body urging the police commissioners to appoint fifty additional police. This resolution was defeated 9–3, and the matter was left entirely to the sheriff. When the sheriff then asked the approval of the police commissioners to appoint the extra men, he was unable to get it. He later attributed this to the fact that one of the commissioners was a Knight and another a sympathizer. Thus the millowners persuaded the sheriff to ask for twenty-three Pinkerton detectives. They arrived on Sunday, July 12, and after meeting with the sheriff were immediately put to work guarding mill properties. As soon as they appeared, the Bay City common council issued a statement to the effect that it viewed "with regret and indignation the introduction into our city of an armed force of alien mercenaries" and asked that the authorities "remove this standing menace from our midst." The millowners, however, felt they were justified in having asked for the Pinkertons. Some hoped to start up their mills again on Monday, and they claimed they had been unable to get protection of their property in any other way.

In the Saginaws, employers also had obstacles to overcome. The Saginaw County sheriff, the Saginaw City police chief, and the captain of the East Saginaw militia were all Knights of Labor. It was also said that the mayor of Saginaw City required a good deal of persuasion to come out on the side of "law and order." When millowners and civic authorities conferred with the sheriff, they did not tell him that they had requested a force of 100 Pinkerton men. They feared that if he knew that, he would refuse to ask the governor to call out the militia as they wanted him to. As it was, the sheriff whittled down the citizen delegation's request for four companies of militia and asked only that the governor activate the two home units. One of these, as already indicated, was headed by a fellow Knight.

The millowners of the Valley found the situation particularly annoying because they believed much of the reticence of the local authorities stemmed from "pure politics." The workingmen in the area, guided by the Knights of Labor there, had been quite successful in recent elections—Barry himself had defeated a millowner in the legislative race. The millowners' hatred for the "outside agitator," by which they meant anyone not employed in the mills, was directed particularly against any officeholder or would-be officeholder who sympathized with the strikers.

The employers suffered further from defections within their own ranks. Three Bay County men announced that they would start their mills on Monday, July 13, at ten hours with full pay. Here, too, the owners claimed political demagoguery. One of the three mills was owned by a Knights candidate for the board of education in the September elections. (He won, as did a majority of the Knights' nominees.)

The millowners had a very important ally, however, in Russell Alger, governor of Michigan. Alger, a wealthy lumberman, came out foursquare for his colleagues. He sent a member of his staff to the Valley when the trouble started and arrived himself on Tuesday, July 14, a week after the strike had begun. He helped persuade the Saginaw County sheriff to ask him for three additional companies of militia. That afternoon, the governor moved on to Bay City. As a result of that visit the governor quickly received requisitions asking for five companies of militia for the Bay City area. Alger expressed shock at the Bay City mayor's sympathy for the strikers, and it was later reported that he "talked business" to the mayor about it. The strikers were quite critical of the governor's behavior in Bay City, for he met privately with the millowners but spoke to the strikers only in a public address, flanked by the wealthiest and most prominent millmen in the county.

Governor Alger's attitude toward the ten-hour legislation can perhaps best be seen from comments he made during an interview he gave to a Detroit newspaperman while the strike was still in progress. The reporter asked if it was true that the managers of Alger's own lumber companies were requesting employees to sign contract forms that amounted to a waiver of the ten-hour law. "I presume it is," he said. "I gave orders to have such contracts sent to our camps." The reporter then asked why the governor had asked that those forms be forwarded. "To have them signed, of course," he replied.

Another newspaper quoted an observer who said that the

governor took strong action in the Valley to avoid trouble "up the shore," in the Au Sable, Oscoda, and Alpena lumber regions where his own lumber interests were located. It was also reported that one reason Governor Alger came to the strike scene was to threaten the Saginaw County sheriff with removal from office unless he arrested Thomas Barry. Barry was duly arrested the day the governor arrived. Bailed out immediately, he was then arrested again and bailed again, just as quickly. In both cases he was charged with violating a Michigan statute, the so-called Baker Conspiracy Law, which prohibited conspiring with others to "willfully and maliciously" interfere with "the regular operations and conduct of the business of any railroad or other corporation, firm or individual." The law reflected a widespread antipathy toward any organized attempt to withhold goods and services, to set prices, or in any way interfere with the "free" working of the economic system. "Trusts" and "monopolies" were deemed unmitigated evils. Concerted action by workers fell under this blanket indictment as an attempt to restrict the operation of the labor market in response to the law of supply and demand. *The New York Times,* editorializing on the Saginaw Valley strike, stated, "All men have an equal right to work, and trying to prevent competition by force savors of the spirit of monopoly." Beyond this, such efforts interfered with the individual worker's freedom to give or withhold his services as he saw fit. The Michigan labor commissioner saw it this way: "The right of a man to 'strike,' quit work, or refuse to go to work, is his. The consequence of such action in its loss to him is his own and he alone is responsible. The right of a man to drive another from his work, or in any way to interfere with his labor, does not exist!"

In all, Barry was arrested six times: five for violating the Baker Conspiracy Law and once on a trespass charge. The total bail amounted to almost $20,000, leading Barry to comment at one point, "I am worth more now than I ever expected to be." Each time, sympathizers pledged bail immediately, and he was free to continue his efforts.

Blinn, too, was arrested, on Wednesday, July 15. In his case, it was harder to find men to put up bail, and he remained in jail for two days. Blinn was not as popular a figure in the

Valley community as Barry. His fiery calls to action had alienated a large portion of the community that was basically sympathetic to the strikers' cause. In contrast, Barry's reasoned appeals to the strikers to avoid violence, forego the pleasures of the saloon, and protect property struck a far more responsive chord. Even the more conservative newspapers covering the strike conceded that there had been little property damage or violence of any kind. They gave Barry much of the credit for this.·

Barry's policy also paid off in terms of the community's attitude toward the strike. The former mayor of East Saginaw probably spoke for much of the Valley when he said, "Our people came out strong for law and order when it looked as though there might be trouble; but there is also a strong undercurrent of feeling that ten hours of work per day is quite enough."

Because of the calm that prevailed, the Pinkerton detectives and militia companies had very little to do. Some Pinkerton men were assigned to guard mills and salt blocks that owners hoped to start up. Others protected nonstrikers as they loaded lumber onto waiting ships, while the militia spent its time drilling or sitting around in the armories.

Much of the Saginaw Valley community shared the Bay City common council's dismay at the presence of the Pinkerton forces. Many felt that these gun-toting "Hessians," as they were often called, would cause more trouble than they would put down. They complained, too, that municipal funds were used to pay the salaries of these outsiders when there were enough men right in the Valley who could be deputized if necessary.

Many residents also questioned the value of keeping the militia around. Not only did it cost the counties money, but many of the militiamen were fraternizing with the strikers and seemed sympathetic to their cause. If there were trouble, how effective would they be? To those who argued that the troops could protect men willing but afraid to work, they pointed out that reprisals were more likely after hours, when the men were at home, than during the workday. Under the circumstances, what effective protection could the troops give them?

The mounting protest was effective, and the governor gradually dismissed the outside forces. The last of them left the evening of July 21. If a millowner requested protection after that, local authorities provided it.

In the meantime, the Knights of Labor had taken another step on behalf of the strikers. After a general meeting on Wednesday, July 15, the organization began to organize relief committees in each of the communities of the Valley. A number of the companies answered the strikers' "ten hours or no sawdust" with "eleven hours or no flour" and closed the company stores to them. The Knights organized stores of their own and gave the strikers rent money. They sent appeals to other local assemblies in the state, their requests were published in the labor newspapers, and on Monday, July 20, the organization held the first of many picnics to help raise money. The Knights persuaded local merchants to make donations and assured the strikers that they would be taken care of as long as they held out. While the Knights of Labor as an organization never officially took over the strike, the aid they extended to the strikers and their families was invaluable. Undoubtedly, it permitted the men to hold out much longer than they otherwise could have.

The millowners were also busy. On July 23 the bulk of the prominent employers in the Valley, representing seventy mills among them, held a joint meeting in East Saginaw. When it was over they issued a resolution stating that they would concede nothing. Although a few mills did start up at ten hours after that statement was issued, in such instances all but the lowest paid workers were forced to take a cut in pay to achieve the shorter workday. However, most of the millowners in the Valley stood firm. The strike had reached a stalemate.

Most of the owners were willing to take the position they did because it was costing them nothing to do so. "My docks and salt sheds are full," said one of them, "and I don't care to run. It would be a benefit to me if the strike did not end for a month." Indeed, except for those with large contracts to fulfill immediately, which accounted for at least some of the breaks in rank, it was proving profitable to remain idle. As lumber and salt became scarce in the Midwest, prices advanced. Good quality lumber sold for as much as $5.00 more per thousand feet at the end of the strike than it had at the beginning. Salt, too, went up in price. The *Lumberman's Gazette* estimated, in early August, that while the strikers were losing $200,000 in wages, the companies were gaining $600,000 due to the rise in prices.

All through the strike, the Saginaw area millowners displayed less willingness to make some sort of compromise with their men than did the Bay City area employers. At one point, it seemed that the strike might actually succeed in the Bay City region. It never looked hopeful downriver. The primary reason for this was the availability of a ready labor supply to any Saginaw employer who wanted to start up his mill. The skilled hands—sawyers, setters, filers, and engineers—in the Saginaw area mills were generally uninterested in the strike. Most of them were not members of the Knights before the strike began and had been idled by it rather than actively praticipating in it. Thus Barry's appeals to them after the strike started were greeted with little enthusiasm. These were key men, and without them, no mill could operate. If they were willing to work, as many of them were, it was then just a matter of finding common labor to fill out the ranks.

Here again, the Saginaw area employers were at an advantage. The so-called boom company, which sorted the logs as they floated down the river, was located near the Saginaws. That company had had to close when the mills shut down. None of its five hundred employees was involved in the strike, and many were anxious to work. Once the skilled workers voiced their willingness to return, the Saginaw employers could then fill in with the boom company men and get back into production. This undoubtedly put pressure on the unskilled millhands in the Saginaw area to return to work themselves, rather than be replaced.

In contrast, in the Bay City region the majority of the skilled men were active supporters of the ten-hour day movement from the beginning and were anxious to hold out until they achieved their aims. The boom company windfall was also unavailable to Bay City employers, and they had to bring in outsiders just to get the lumber off the docks.

Once it was clear that the Saginaw employers had the upper hand in their area, the Bay City millowners were less ready to settle with their own employees on terms that would have been completely disadvantageous. As mills reopened in the Saginaws, the Bay City employers let it be known that they would ship their logs up the river to the Saginaws rather than concede.

On July 29, in the fourth week of the strike, the Knights' Grand Master Workman, Terence Powderley, visited the strike scene. While he made no public statement, he privately urged all workers getting more than $1.50 a day to accept a cut in daily wages in order to attain a ten-hour day and get back to work. By early August most strikers would have been more than happy to go back on those terms.

Barry was incensed when the workers were willing to retreat from their original position and compromise with their employers; and he must have been equally irritated with Powderley for encouraging that attitude. Barry broke with Powderley two years later, over what he considered a betrayal in another strike, and formed a short-lived rival organization of his own. After Powderley's visit to the Valley, however, Barry said nothing, at least in public.

From Powderley's point of view, the Saginaw Valley strike was just one of many disputes in which his organization was either directly or indirectly involved at the time. Powderley's advice also reflected his own cautious approach to employee-employer disputes, his aversion to strikes, and his willingness to accept small gains won over time, rather than to make an all-out fight.

The Grand Master Workman's caution also reflected the amorphous character of the Knights of Labor. Apparently not all the local assemblies in the Valley were happy with the Knights' efforts to aid the strikers. Six of the local units in East Saginaw specifically asked Powderley to be detached from that district assembly and to be placed directly under the General Assembly's jurisdiction. At least one local assembly in the state that contributed to the strike relief fund asked to be excused from another assessment the national body was levying at the time because it had insufficient funds to do both.

To Powderley, then, the Saginaw Valley strike was damaging his organization's image, splitting its structure, and draining its treasury. It is, therefore, not surprising that he urged the men to go back to work.

As the strikers' position deteriorated, further violence erupted. Strikers shut down mills and salt blocks by force and threatened those who had gone back to work. Local authorities also adopted a tougher policy. In the second week of August, Saginaw police charged into a group of strikers who were trying to close a mill. The policemen swung their clubs in all directions, injuring many severely and arresting five. The next week, the Essexville marshall, the Bay County sheriff, and a number of deputies dispersed another group, which had just shut down a salt block, by firing upon them, wounding four. This time, nine were arrested, and the local militia was called up again.

Throughout August, more and more mills opened, most of them at eleven hours a day. Any owner who agreed to ten hours required a cut in daily wages for all but the lowest paid. Mills that had originally granted ten hours at full pay now backed down.

Only the lowest-paid employees—those making less than $1.25 or $1.50 a day, depending on the mill—were making any gains at all as a consequence of the strike, which probably added to its weakening. Those with higher earnings would see no reason to hold out. It may be significant that the millowners announced in early October that they planned to hire no immigrant labor during the 1886 milling season. Perhaps the "Polanders" were the backbone of the strike at the end, as they were at the beginning.

By the beginning of September the Great Strike had disintegrated, and almost all of the mills in the Valley were running again. Some of the millowners had promised their workers that if they came back at eleven hours, the ten-hour law would be observed once it went into effect. Instead, when the time came, the employers asked the men to sign the contracts necessary to avoid the law. This caused a flurry of short strikes, but within a week the strikers were either back on the employers' terms or had been replaced. With the milling season almost at an end, employment dwindled in the mills, and prospects for work in the woods were poor. Enthusiasm for ten hours was more than offset by the prospect of the grim winter ahead.

The following spring, as the mills began to reopen, a notice appeared in the labor papers saying: "Wageworkers are requested to keep away from the Saginaw Valley until the labor troubles are settled. It is possible that an attempt will be made to run 11 or 12 hours, despite the 10-hour law." The notice did no good, apparently, because a majority of the mills ran at eleven hours or more during the 1886 season.

There were no more strikes for the ten-hour day in the Saginaw Valley. The forests in the area had already been greatly depleted by some forty years of lumbering and, even in 1885, lumbermen brought in logs from as far away as the Upper Peninsula. A few years later the mills were tapping the Canadian forests. The Valley's huge stands of virgin white pine had been demolished. As transportation costs made continued use of distant forests too unprofitable, the mills closed down one by one. The fires were put out under the salt blocks, this time permanently.

The lumberjacks moved on to sing of other forests. The millmen would have to fight for their rights somewhere else. In the Saginaw Valley, "ten hours or no sawdust" lingered only as a memory.

3

THE SECOND BATTLE
OF BATTLE CREEK

In the opening years of the twentieth century, the American labor movement cordially despised Battle Creek, Michigan. It scorned the town's leading citizen, C. W. Post, of cereal fame, with equal fervor. Organized labor was then in the middle of an uphill battle against the so-called open shop movement. Post represented one of the movement's most vocal advocates, and Battle Creek was a model open shop town.

Neither the town nor the man had always been so hostile to trade unionism. A labor organizer recalled nostalgically that in 1895 Battle Creek was "the best organized town of its size in the country." Nor is there any evidence that would indicate that Post had any particular quarrel with organized labor before 1901. The change in attitude reflected a reaction throughout the country to the American Federation of Labor's spectacular rise to power.

When it was formed in 1886, the AFL could count no more than 140,000 members. In 1904, less than twenty years later, the organization, through its 120 affiliated unions, had a membership of 1,676,000.

Samuel Gompers, the Federation's first President, deserves much of the credit for the organization's success. Labor historian Foster Rhea Dulles records that as soon as Gompers was elected, he set up

> headquarters in an eight-by-ten foot office made available by the Cigar Makers, with little furniture other than a kitchen table, some crates for chairs, and a filing case made out of tomato boxes, [and] . . . set about breathing vitality into the new organization with a zeal, devotion and tireless energy that largely accounted for its survival. He wrote innumerable letters, always in his own hand, to labor leaders throughout the country; for a time edited the *Trade Union Advocate* as a means of publicizing his campaign; issued union charters, collected dues, handled all routine business; managed conventions and went on speaking and organization tours, and slowly but persistently transformed the American Federation of Labor from a purely paper organization into a militant and powerful champion of labor's rights. He felt himself to be engaged in a holy cause and from the day the A.F. of L. came into being until his death thirty-eight years later, it was his entire life.*

From the start, Gompers emphasized that AFL unions should concentrate on immediate economic gains to be won at the bargaining table. Yet from the beginning, member unions also engaged in political activity. Gompers insisted, however, that such activity be strictly nonpartisan. Labor would support its friends and defeat its enemies without regard to party label. It would not become tied to any one party nor take ·independent political action.

The early years were not easy ones for the AFL. Not only was it struggling to defeat the Knights of Labor, but, particularly during the depression that lasted from 1893 to 1896, it had to fight off attempts by the socialists and others to use is as a

---

* Foster Rhea Dulles, *Labor in America,* 3rd ed., New York, Thomas Y. Crowell, 1966, p. 162.

political vehicle. Nonetheless, the AFL was the victor on both fronts before the close of the nineteenth century.

As the nation's economy recovered after 1896, employers, anxious to keep production moving, were willing to deal with the organizations that represented their skilled help, hoping to assure a stable work force and to avoid strikes. Wages began a steady climb. In Michigan, for example, the average wage earner in a factory or workshop took home $1.77 a day by 1904, as compared to $1.23 in 1896, an increase of almost 45 percent in eight years. Wages for skilled workers were even higher. Moreover, the average worker was employed more days in a year in 1904 than in 1896.

In that atmosphere, labor unions grew and flourished. Though Michigan was still primarily agricultural, and the growth in trade unionism in the state was not as great as in

Samuel Gompers, first president of the American Federation of Labor

more highly industrialized areas, union membership did rise perceptibly. In 1898 canvassers for the state's Bureau of Labor and Industrial Statistics counted 10,308 union members in 111 organizations. In 1902 the number had nearly tripled. That year the Bureau men received data from over 300 labor unions with almost 27,000 members and estimated that probably another 200 organizations with an additional 13,000 members did not participate in the canvass. Detroit unions alone reported over 10,000 members in 1902—an increase of over 2,000 in just one year. The following year 589 locals with 43,609 members filed reports. But in Michigan, as everywhere else, the honeymoon was soon over. Organized labor's very success became cause for alarm, and a reaction set in.

The number of strikes increased dramatically throughout the nation in the early years of the twentieth century. In 1898 the U. S. Commissioner of Labor reported 1,056 strikes; by 1903 the figure stood at 3,494. Public sympathy toward labor unions eroded as the effects of such stoppages impinged more and more on average American citizens' daily lives. In those years, when the automobile was still a rich man's toy, a stranded public became increasingly annoyed every time the streetcar employees struck or the deliverymen went out. One teamsters strike in Chicago threatened to tie up the whole city. Building trades strikes in Chicago and New York brought construction to a standstill. Subsequent allegations of corruption among union leaders involved in some of the stoppages further hardened public sentiment.

In addition, the public considered wage increases at least partly to blame for the noticeable inflation of those years. What cost just over $.72 in 1897 was priced at over $1.00 by 1902, a jump of close to 39 percent in six years. The average consumer felt himself caught in a squeeze between the greed for profits of the "Corporate Trusts" and the zealous wage demands of the "Labor Trust."

The segment of the American public that was the most outraged at the increase in union power was, not surprisingly, the employers. One object of their disapproval was organized labor's use of the boycott. Like the Knights of Labor before them, the AFL affiliates used that weapon effectively to pressure employers into granting them recognition. Unions not only instituted boycotts against manufacturers whom they deemed "unfair" but also against those who sought to sell or use the offending manufacturers' products. The AFL helped to publicize such efforts in the "We Don't Patronize" columns, which were a feature of its widely circulated monthly magazine, the *American Federationist*.

Employers had other reasons for their dissatisfaction with trade unions. Despite Gompers' emphasis upon the sanctity of contracts, the increasing number of strikes made it obvious that a signed labor agreement was not foolproof insurance against a walkout. Equally irksome, once such an agreement had been signed, the union wanted a voice in matters that went beyond immediate wage issues: when and how employees were to be paid, how long they would work and how much they should produce in that time, how many apprentices could be hired, the type of machinery that could be used, who could be fired, and so on. As one Detroit manufacturer put it after successfully ousting the union from his own concern, "The unionists have attempted to run our business for us, but we propose to do that ourselves."

A recurrent union demand was for the so-called closed shop, which required that a man be a union member before he could be hired. Employer resistance eventually crystallized around this issue in what came to be called the open shop movement.

The movement found favor not only among employers of the nation. President Theodore Roosevelt reflected widespread public sentiment when in 1903 he ended a closed shop agreement in the Government Printing Office that had existed for over forty years. "There is no objection to employes of the government forming or belonging to unions, but the government can neither discriminate for nor discriminate against nonunion men who are in its employment or who seek to be employed under it," he explained. The judiciary fortified Roosevelt's position. Increasingly, the courts ruled the closed shop illegal.

A government-appointed mediation commission in Michigan summarized the reasons for the growing hostility to organized labor:

When unions, so helpful along many lines, undertake to
curtail the liberties of individual men, be they employer or
employed, shutting up one to the necessity of securing a
certain kind of help and the other to working or idling as
they may elect, they pass all bounds of reason and become
enemies of the best social order. All violence in time of
strikes, the setting upon non-union men because they
choose not to become members of the organization, crying
"scab," instituting the boycott, are all agents of tyranny,
foreign to the genius of American liberty.

The president of Harvard University went so far as to intimate
that the real American hero was the strikebreaker, the "independent workingman" unwilling to follow the dictates of organized labor.

The employers involved in the open shop movement won
wide support because publicly they posed as defenders of individual liberty. They echoed President Roosevelt and advocated
that no man should be discriminated against because he was or
was not a union member. For many of them, however, the true
purpose of the movement was to be rid of unions altogether.

The open shop movement began simultaneously on various
fronts in 1901. U. S. Steel began the drive to rid its plants of
labor organizations. The Metal Trades Association, which had
been bargaining with the International Association of Machinists, announced after a strike call that it would no longer deal
with that union. A newly formed employers association in Dayton, Ohio, initiated a citywide campaign to make Dayton an
open shop town. By the following year a number of other cities,
Chicago among them, were following Dayton's example. Detroit
jumped on the bandwagon in 1903. Smaller towns established
more broadly based organizations, usually called "citizens alliances," to accomplish the same purpose.

Some of the manufacturers who were on the AFL "unfair"
list in 1902 formed a secret society, the American Anti-Boycott
Association. Its purpose was to fight boycotts through the
courts. The National Association of Manufacturers, hitherto
concerned mostly with tariffs, also entered the fight. Its 1903
convention was largely devoted to the labor question. A "Dec-

laration of Principles," which served as a rallying point for all open shop advocates, emerged from that meeting.

The declaration listed union activity that the NAM opposed—strikes, boycotts, interference in the conduct of business—and singled out the closed shop demand for special attention. It was, among other things, "an invasion of the constitutional rights of the American workman." The association then pledged itself "to oppose any and all legislation not in accord with the foregoing declaration."

Despite NAM avowal that it was an apolitical body, its pledge to oppose certain legislation led it to take a closer look at the legislators who might vote for or against it. Thus, like the AFL, the NAM was soon urging its members to reward friends and punish enemies. By the 1906 congressional elections, the NAM and AFL were battling it out in the political arena. The following year the NAM created a separate department, the National Council for Industrial Defense, to carry on its political activities. In the 1908 presidential campaign, the "apolitical" NAM backed the Republican candidate, Taft, as vigorously as the "nonpartisan" AFL supported his opponent, Bryan.

Aside from the concerted political efforts of the NAM, individual employers used many ways to rid their own plants of unionism. A few used strong-arm methods. Companies stationed guards at the plant entrances to turn away union men and employed thugs to rough up union leaders. If violence broke out, the employer called in the local police. At times, state or federal troops were also called in. Almost invariably, the uniformed men came not as neutrals interested solely in restoring peace, but as allies of the employer. In short, they usually functioned as "union busters."

Once a union had been ousted, the employer often required his workers to sign a pledge that they would not join a union while they worked for him,—union men often referred to such pledges as "yellow-dog" contracts—and plants hired spies to ensure that that promise was kept.

More common was what came to be known as "welfare capitalism" or "industrial betterment," a system under which the employer gave to his employees voluntarily what a union might presumably have won through bargaining, had there been a union. As a part of their "industrial betterment" program, employers often established "company unions" or "shop committees" to serve as sounding boards for employee grievances.

With this combination of methods, the open shop movement moved ahead rapidly. Union membership ceased to grow, and then declined. By 1909 AFL membership stood at under 1,500,-000—a drop of almost 200,000 in five years. The antiunion campaign made some headway in the larger cities, but its greatest successes were in the smaller urban centers of the country: Joliet, Illinois; Dayton, Ohio; Beloit, Wisconsin.

Battle Creek was another triumph for open shop advocates. In their eyes the town was doubly blessed because it housed C. W. Post, a prominent figure in the NAM and a charter member of the Citizens' Industrial Association of America. That association was an NAM-inspired body created in 1903 to forge local citizens alliances and employer associations into a national organization. Post served as its president from 1905 until it merged with the National Council for Industrial Defense at the end of 1908.

Post viewed the open shop movement as a fight for freedom and justice. When he addressed the delegates to the 1903 NAM convention, his words were those of a crusader exhorting the righteous to band together to smite down evil:

> I come to . . . plead the cause of human liberty in its struggle against tyranny, force and oppression, those old enemies of mankind. . . .
>
> The manufacturers of this country must organize. They have a duty to perform that they cannot shirk. That duty lies toward the innocent children made fatherless by the tyranny of union laborers; toward the wives made widows from the same cause; toward the small tradesman throughout the country, whose business has been ruined; toward the manufacturers whose property has been destroyed . . . toward the country at large whose people are threatened with the loss of prosperity and that thing dearest to the human soul—liberty. . . .

Anarchy, tyranny, mob violence and murder must and shall be put down.

There is no reason to doubt that Post sincerely believed that he was engaged in a battle of "right" against "might"; he was not merely mouthing platitudes. He showed a concern for the welfare of his own workers: he never used strong-arm methods against them to keep unions from his door but relied solely upon the principles of welfare capitalism to hold their loyalty.

At the same time, however, Post had a well-developed sense of the force of the profit motive, and it is sometimes difficult to separate self-interest from principle in assessing his actions. While this is particularly true in attempting to evaluate Post's dealings with his own employees, it also holds for other aspects of Post's involvement with the open shop movement.

Post was the founder of the Postum Cereal Company, which

C. W. Post

manufactured Postum (a coffee substitute), Grape Nuts, and Post Toasties. His company had never been unionized, so during the first years of the open shop fight in Battle Creek his own plants were not involved. Others among the town's employers, particularly the threshing machine and steam pump factories, led the local battle. Post himself entered the movement first at the national level.

His initial involvement was the result of the nationwide advertising campaigns he carried on to acquaint the American public with the wonders of his breakfast foods. The Los Angeles *Times*, a newspaper that regularly carried Post's material, was a leading open shop advocate. In 1901, after successfully ridding itself of the International Typographical Union (ITU), the paper spearheaded a citywide open shop drive. In response, the ITU sent out letters to all the paper's advertisers, including Post, and asked them to withdraw their business from the *Times*. Post refused. In accordance with its policy in such cases, the union then listed him and his products in labor papers throughout the country and urged readers to write letters of protest to Post and to boycott his cereals. Post responded to the mail barrage by buying newspaper space all over the country and filling it with denunciations of such tactics. In one such ad he threatened: "If the great buying public decides to obey the orders of the labor unions, and refuse to purchase our products, we have but one thing to do—go out of business and let the families dependent on that business go adrift and shift for themselves. ... We cannot and will not join the conspiracy of these labor unions to ruin publishers."

Thereafter, antiunion blasts frequently appeared under his signature in many of the nation's newspapers. Any publications that refused to print what he called his "educational" material soon found that it had lost the Postum Cereal Company advertising account as well. Post also called attention to such offenders in the monthly magazine, *The Square Deal*, the voice of the Citizens' Industrial Association of America. While Post might decry a union's use of the boycott weapon, he did not hesitate to use it himself.

Post's products never reached the *American Federationist*'s "We Don't Patronize" columns since no union ever gained a sufficient foothold in his plant to be able to charge that it was being dealt with unfairly. However, once Post became president of the Citizens' Industrial Association, he himself appeared on the list under "Miscellaneous." Presumably, he personally could be considered unfair to the American labor movement as a whole.

Post remained on the list until the February 1908 issue of the magazine, the last to carry a "We Don't Patronize" column. The column's disappearance signaled a major victory for the open shop forces and reflected the effect of two recent court decisions. One of these, the Supreme Court's decision in the *Danbury Hatters* case, held that a boycott instituted by the United Hatters of North America against a Danbury, Connecticut, hat manufacturer was a combination in restraint of trade within the meaning of the Sherman Antitrust Act. Furthermore, it was later determined that not only the union as an organization and its officers but all members of the union were financially liable for the damages due the company under the act.

The second case hit directly at the *American Federationist's* "unfair" list and arose out of a metal polishers strike against the Buck's Stove & Range Company of St. Louis. The company president, James Van Cleave, personified the open shop movement. He was president of the NAM, vice-president of the Citizens' Industrial Association, chairman of the National Council for Industrial Defense, and a member of the Anti-Boycott Association.

After the metal polishers struck Van Cleave's firm, the stove company was added to the AFL's "We Don't Patronize" listing. Van Cleave then obtained a court injunction to have his company's name taken off the list. The injunction not only prohibited the magazine from keeping the stove company on the list, but also enjoined AFL officials from making any reference to the company or taking any action in any way that might be construed as a boycott or the threat of one. Gompers was outraged. He called the injunction "the most sweeping ever issued," and labeled it "an invasion of the liberty of the press and the right of free speech." When he and other AFL officials persisted in calling attention to the company and its labor problems, they were cited for contempt of court and sentenced to jail.

The AFL immediately appealed both the injunction and the contempt citation.

Gompers had already been campaigning for national legislation to free unions from "government by injunction," and he now redoubled his efforts: "The unions of labor will live. They can not be—they must not be driven out of existence. Labor demands relief at the hands of Congress; demands it NOW."

In 1910, just before the Buck's Stove cases were to be argued before the Supreme Court, Van Cleave died. His successor, Fred Gardiner, immediately made overtures to the AFL to settle out of court. The company's business had dropped off by 40 percent since the beginning of its antiunion campaign, and Gardiner was more concerned with that than in continuing his predecessor's open shop fight. The company dropped the injunction case and signed a labor agreement. (The contempt case was eventually dismissed on a technicality.) Post, a stockholder in the Buck's Stove Company, did everything he could to prevent Gardiner from reversing Van Cleave. When he saw that persuasion was futile, Post tried to get an injunction to prohibit the company from signing the contract with the union. When that also failed, he instituted proceedings, as an aggrieved stockholder, to compel the company officials to prosecute a damage suit against the AFL under the Sherman Act. This too came to nothing.

Post's activities exasperated Gompers. In an editorial on "Post, Cheap Mischief Maker," he wrote: "And now the question arises, what will labor, its friends and sympathizers do under the circumstances? Let Post wither in the narrowing circle in which he moves, or refuse to give their patronage to his Potsum, Gripe Nuts and Toatsies? There have been instances when men of the type of Post, bearing other names, have felt the result of the people's wrath against a common-scold, a malevolent mischief maker or a public enemy." While Gompers did not exactly tell his readers to boycott Post's products, it was a very strong hint.

Gompers also asserted that Post was carrying on at such great length chiefly to get free publicity for his products. He may well have been right. According to Leo Wolman, an authority on the union boycott, the market for Post's products was largely confined to the middle class, a segment of American society already largely antiunion. Thus while a boycott ordinarily cut into a company's business, Post's well-publicized open shop efforts actually helped his sales.

Post had also become involved in open shop efforts in Battle Creek itself. The background for that involvement was a cereal "boom" that was in full swing in Battle Creek by 1902 largely as a result of Post's own successes with his breakfast foods. When Post arrived in Battle Creek in 1891, the town was not yet a world-famous center of ready-to-eat breakfast cereal. Instead, its most important industries were the threshing machine and steam pump factories mentioned earlier. The town was best known as the world headquarters of the Seventh Day Adventists, and particularly for the Adventist's health resort, the Battle Creek Sanitarium.

The man who had done the most to establish the "San's" reputation was its director, Dr. John Kellogg, the older brother of W. K. Kellogg, whose signature would appear on millions of cereal boxes some years later. "Dr. John" combined medical knowledge, an enthusiasm for various health fads, and a gift for self-advertisement. With those requisites, he put the San on the map. Those who could afford the price came from all over the country to partake of Dr. Kellogg's vegetarian diet, substitute coffee, and restful atmosphere. They took salt rubs, ran barefoot through the morning dew, and listened to the doctor's lectures on such uplifting topics as the need for thorough mastication. Typically, Sanitarium guests were not hopelessly ill. They simply suffered the effects of the then-standard American diet, heavily weighted toward fried foods liberally doused with floured gravies. When the San guests arrived, they were usually overweight and "dyspeptic." When they left they often had shed some pounds—there were only two meals a day at the San—and felt better. Their stomachs were silent; their livers quiescent. Then after another year of the usual greasy, lumpy fare, they were again ready for Dr. Kellogg's ministrations.

It was the Sanitarium that atracted C. W. Post to Battle Creek. He was in failing health and hopeful that Dr. Kellogg's program would make him well again.

Limited quantities of the various meat and drink substitutes—

including peanut butter—that emerged from Dr. Kellogg's laboratory and Mrs. Kellogg's test kitchen were produced for sale, but the doctor never tried to develop a wide market for them. The rest of the medical profession would have frowned on such activity and, in any event, the doctor had too many other interests. The potential for a mass market was there, however, and it only required a man of C. W. Post's interests and abilities to take advantage of it. As soon as he was well, Post began concocting health foods of his own.

The first of his products was a coffee substitute, Postum, which he placed on the market in 1895. As soon as it was ready for sale, Post set about advertising it on a scale hitherto unknown in connection with foodstuffs and in terms that differed considerably from the modest, low-key phraseology associated with food ads. "If coffee don't agree, use Postum," said one. This, Post said, was "plain words for plain people". His ads also warned against "coffee neuralgia" and assured the public that Postum would "feed and rebuild the nerve centres broken down by coffee and other stimulants." Postum also "made red blood" and, according to its inventor, saved marriages.

In 1898 Post launched the breakfast cereal Grape Nuts, which, said the ads, was "partially predigested" and would thus not overtax the digestive organs "in cases of derangement of stomach and bowels." Post's emphasis upon visceral malfunctions earned him the title of "the Henry Ford of the alimentary canal." At the same time, his claims attracted a segment of the American public that was suffering as acutely from its dietary habits as were those who attended the fashionable health resorts, but who could not afford either the time or the entrance fee. Post's products benefitted too from the widespread public alarm over the disclosures that finally led to the passage of the Pure Food and Drug Act of 1906. The fact that Post's products were not branded as "impure" was very much in their favor.

Consumer response to Post's ads was tremendous, and by 1901 Post was clearing nearly a million dollars a year. Two years later he was estimated to be worth ten million dollars.

Inevitably, Post's earnings attracted a host of imitators. Because of the Sanitarium and the Postum Cereal Company,

Battle Creek had become so closely identified with health and "pure food" that no matter where a cereal company was established, "Battle Creek" was likely to appear somewhere in its title. It was better yet to be able to print "made in Battle Creek" on every package.

In the first few years of the twentieth century, the town took on such a bonanza atmosphere that it made national headlines. Over forty cereal companies were established in and around Battle Creek during the period. They seemed to spring up overnight, making housing so tight that tent colonies mushroomed on any available vacant space.

Although labor flocked into the town from all over the state, workers were still in short supply. The regional AFL organizer thought that now, at last, he could get a foothold in that model open shop town, but his dreams were short-lived. The only cereal company he managed to organize, while advertising itself as a Battle Creek company, was actually located in Yorkville, some sixteen miles away. The firm advertised that it was "a fearless advocate of the union label," but even that did not win labor over to its "peptonized and celery impregnated" product, Tryabita. Like Malta Vita, Grain-O, Force, Cero-Fruito, Strengtho, and a score of other cereals, Tryabita shortly disappeared from the American breakfast table.

The AFL organizer's efforts had little impact upon the Postum Cereal Company, although there is a notation in the company's payroll records that one man actually threatened to strike. He was discharged at once. Post's policy was firm: "We have discouraged Labor Unions, and, in fact, do not permit a union man to have employment in our works, for the simple reason that under the rule of modern labor unions, we could not obtain the same faithfulness from our employees as we do at present." Post ran his own kind of closed shop.

As indicated earlier, Post's policies toward his workers contained many elements of "enlightened paternalism," although much tempered by his keen eye for the profit margin. Post's detractors declared that he made every dollar raise another. He himself said he helped a man to help himself. There is an element of truth in both statements.

Before the cereal boom, the Postum Cereal Company payroll

records indicate that Post was a hard taskmaster. But once his would-be competitors began flocking to Battle Creek, Post began applying "welfare capitalism" principles in his own company and urged other employers to follow his example. He told his colleagues that they should pay good wages and often boasted that his town paid the highest rates in the state—something of an exaggeration. He criticized the practice of lowering piece rates as employees became more proficient and productive. He himself had been guilty of that earlier. In late August 1897, for example, Post cut the rate per barrel of roasted bran—used in manufacturing Postum—from $.70 to $.60. At the same time he lowered the rate for packing cereal cartons. Boxes which had brought $.25 per 100 were reduced to $.22; those which had paid $.20 moved to $.15. When Post began manufacturing Grape Nuts, in January 1898, he paid $.18 per 100 for packaging the cereal. Six months later, he reduced the rate to $.14 per 100.

Once the boom began in Battle Creek, however, Post stopped tinkering with piece rates—at least so far as his male employees were concerned. The men also got substantial wage boosts, less stringent work rules, and a lenient time-off policy. Fines for poor work or tardiness were also eliminated.

The women in Post's employ did not fare so well. They held the less skilled jobs, were less mobile, and not as likely to be the object of a labor organizer's wiles. While the weekly rate for men ranged between $9.90 and $15.00, women generally continued to average somewhere between $4.50 and $6.50, as they had before the boom began. Fines were still levied vigorously against female employees, and their piece rates moved up and down, and down some more, as usual. Insubordination brought not only discharge for women, but blacklisting.

Post opposed the building of libraries or bath houses for his workers, a common "industrial betterment" feature. He maintained that if a firm paid high wages any employee who wanted a book or a bath could get it himself, in his own way. Post was also uninterested in profit sharing, another common "welfare capitalism" scheme. Yearly profits varied, he said, and could be nonexistent in any given year. Profit sharing just led to false hopes and dissatisfaction.

Post's own efforts centered around providing homes for employees and a bonus plan. He had been selling lots to employees on the installment plan before the housing shortage developed in Battle Creek, and in 1901 he went into the real estate business on a grand scale. He bought 80 acres adjacent to his plant, divided the land into 33' x 128' lots and built houses of from five to seven rooms on them. The house and lot together were priced at anywhere from $975 to $3600, and employees who had been with Post for a year or more could buy them on time, at 1 percent of the total cost per month. If the full price was $1,000, the monthly payment was $10.00, and so on.

Post decided who could afford what house: "Sometimes the ambitions of a proud wife had to be curbed and her hopes, of far outshining her neighbors of like earning capacity, destroyed. No workman could purchase a home beyond his means,

The Grape Nuts packing room circa 1901

and about 20 percent of his earnings was considered the limit.
... He could not purchase a more expensive property unless he
could show financial resources outside his wages." Given the
minimum price of his homes, the 20 percent rule effectively
eliminated the lowest paid employees from consideration as
potential homeowners. Post made it clear that he made a profit
on the land itself but said that he sold the houses at cost. The
total selling price, however, included 6 percent annual interest.
Furthermore, contrary to Post's assertion, the monthly payments
were not less than comparable rentals in the town.

He never publicly connected his housing scheme with the
bonus system he instituted two years later; but the way the
system operated leads to the speculation, at least, that it may
have been a means of encouraging workers to buy one of the
homes. The bonus plan went into effect in July 1903 when the
following notice was posted:

> All factory employes of this company that have been in
> *CONTINUOUS* service one year, will receive each week a
> bonus of 5% added to the regular wages, after July 1,
> 1903. Employes that have been in *CONTINUOUS* service
> two years, will receive a bonus of 10% added to the
> regular wages, after July 1, 1903. This rule will apply to
> employes as soon as they reach the one or two year stan-
> dard. Absence for thirty days caused by sickness or by
> permission of the company will not count as a break in the
> service. ...
>
> /s/ H. E. Burt, Superintendent
> By order of C. W. POST

At the same time, the salaried office force, which did not come
under the bonus system, was given sick leave benefits: full pay
for the first three weeks, half pay for the next five. "Anything
over two months *no pay*." By that time the salaried force also
received a week's paid vacation after a year's service. Those eligible for a 5 percent bonus did not receive it in their weekly
paychecks. It was banked instead. As Post explained, "we want
to give him a practical illustration of the fact that he can live
through the year on the same amount of wages that he has been

accustomed to and save this extra money without feeling it." At the end of the year he was given the bank passbook.

During the first five years of the bonus plan, those entitled to 10 percent received only half of it in cash. The other half was put in the bank. Beginning in 1909 that practice was discontinued, and once an employee became entitled to 10 percent, the full amount appeared in his weekly paycheck.

The company continued to pay the bonus after the 1901-04 boom ended in Battle Creek, but the wages on which it was based varied considerably, depending on company successes in the cereal market. While the bonus continued, the end of the cereal bonanza affected employee relations in other ways. As soon as it was over, a new fine appeared: $.25 for failing to punch the time clock on arriving or leaving. This applied to everyone and was levied vigorously. The company began tinkering with the piece rates for its male employees again, too.

Post administered "industrial betterment" principles very carefully in practice, and with all due consideration for the profit margin. In fairness to him, however, it should be noted that Post was not exceptional in this regard. Workers became wary of "welfare capitalism" precisely because it usually worked the way it did at the Postum Cereal Company.

Worker housing was not the only real estate venture Post undertook in Battle Creek in the early 1900s. He bought and built up business blocks, and erected a sugar factory, a creamery, a box and carton firm, the Post Tavern (a hotel), and large office buildings. He also purchased a large amount of other land in and around the city. His various enterprises made him the largest employer in the county by 1904, and, as one observer noted, Battle Creek was "very close to a one-man town."*

Post thus had a very heavy investment in Battle Creek's future. When the boom was over, he also had a considerable amount of vacant real estate on his hands. To offset this, Post began offering free factory sites to firms that would establish themselves in the

* Today Battle Creek is more often associated with W. K. Kellogg than with C. W. Post. Kellogg, however, did not go into business for himself until 1906, and his firm, in terms of payroll size, did not begin to rival the Postum Cereal Company until after Post's death in 1914. Post's other interests in and around Battle Creek put him far ahead of his potential rival, in any event.

town. It was also at this point that he took an active hand in the Battle Creek open shop drive. He advertised widely that Battle Creek was an open shop town and, in 1904, organized a citizens' alliance to ensure that it stayed that way. Unions may have had hard going in Battle Creek before, but now, as one labor paper put it, "a union man is practically a marked man."

At its 1908 convention the AFL delegates finally turned their attention to C. W. Post and his town, as they considered the following resolution:

> WHEREAS, There is no city or section of the country where organized labor is in a more deplorable and terrorized condition than in Battle Creek, Mich., the home of C. W. Post; and
>
> WHEREAS, A few brave union men are standing together and fighting for their rights in spite of a strong combination against them, captained by one of the greatest enemies of organized labor in this country; therefore, be it
>
> RESOLVED, That the attention of the American Federation of Labor in Convention assembled ... is called to the unorganized condition of the workers of that city, and that some effort be made to send organizers of the American Federation of Labor, as well as organizers of the various internationals, to that city. ...

The resolution, in slightly amended form, was referred to the executive council for its "earliest attention."

The organizing drive did not get underway until 1910 and reached its peak at a bad time, just after the dynamiting of the Los Angeles *Times* building. Twenty people were killed and an additional seventeen injured in the explosion. The dynamiting was generally attributed to that newspaper's antiunionism although the AFL initially denied that there was any connection. Eventually it proved to be the work of some members of the Iron Workers Union, an AFL affiliate.

Public reaction to the dynamiting reached near hysteria and when Gompers came to address a meeting in Battle Creek, as a part of the organizing drive, he was very much on the defen-sive.

The Battle Creek employers had been thoroughly alerted to the impending invasion of union organizers in any event. The pages of Post's *The Square Deal* and his daily newspaper, the Battle Creek *Enquirer,* were full of warnings and exhortations. And it seems that the words were heeded, although it could, of course, be mere coincidence that wages for male workers in Battle Creek jumped noticeably between 1909 and 1910. In one year, their daily pay went from an average of $2.37 to $2.69. In 1910 Battle Creek actually made good Post's boast that it paid the highest wages in the state to men, though the year before it had ranked only tenth among the forty leading cities in the state; by 1911 it had dropped back to fifth. Women benefitted too when their average daily wage rose to $1.37 in 1910 from $1.31 the year before.

The AFL's organizing drive failed. Labor leaders might call Battle Creek "a running sore on the face of the earth and a scab on the map of Michigan," but the town proudly continued to advertise "the Battle Creek Way" to peaceful labor relations and to invite the rest of the country to emulate it.

Post always insisted that he was not against labor organizations in theory; he only disliked the existing ones. In 1910, when the AFL was conducting its drive in Battle Creek, and probably as a consequence of it, Post created a labor organization of which he could approve. He conceived of his National Trades and Workers Association as more than a company union, limited to his employees alone. It was intended to be a nationwide competitor to the hated Labor Trust. He described the nature of his creation: "It does not countenance strikes, boycotts, picketing, lockouts or any form of coercion in the relation between employers and employees. It relies solely upon mediation and public opinion for the settlement of differences regarding wages, hours and conditions." Those joining the organization were required to sign what was in effect a "no-strike" pledge.

All disputes were to be settled by a board of mediation, composed of an equal number of employer and employee representatives, as well as neutrals: "In case employers refuse to abide by the finding of the board of mediation the workingmen have a right to quit, 5 percent of the membership per day. They can seek new employment, but are not permitted to interfere with the men taking their places or coerce employees in any manner." In addition, in case no settlement could be reached, the board of mediation was to publish the recommendations it had made, and public opinion was expected to pressure the employers into accepting them: "the effect on the employers' business will be so marked that they will be glad to make all the reasonable and just concessions asked by their workmen." Post admitted that this had all the earmarks of a boycott, but it was one inaugurated "by the people at large, influenced by their highest sense of justice," and thus was "the finest and most powerful weapon of civilization."

In a dramatic gesture, so typical of Post, he announced that the presidency of the new organization would be offered to former President Theodore Roosevelt for a year, at a salary of $100,000 to be paid by Post personally. What would happen after the first year would depend upon the circumstances, he said. Post knew Roosevelt and admired him, and there is no reason to suppose that he would not have been delighted had Roosevelt accepted the offer. One is led to wonder, however, if he would not also have been very much surprised.

In any event, Roosevelt declined and Joseph Bryce, identified by Post as "at one time president of the state association of railroad trainmen," served instead. The Battle Creek *Enquirer* explained that the fact that Bryce was then vice-president of the Battle Creek Industrial Association, successor to the earlier citizens' alliance, "has nothing to do with the new organization."

Post gave his association a 300-room health resort to be used for the organization's "helpless and infirm." This gift received wide publicity at the time as an outstanding example of Post's philanthropic bent, and President Taft even made a detour in order to have a look at it. The building was a product of the boom days. One of the short-lived cereal companies had expanded into the health resort business. When the company went bankrupt Post picked up the vacant sanitarium building at auction. He first rented it to the physical fitness addict Bernarr McFadden, who ran a health resort there for a few years. It stood empty after McFadden left until Post gave it to the Trades and Workers Association.

The gift was a source of unending problems for the association. The bulk of the dues collected by the national office had to be set aside to maintain the place, and there was never enough in the treasury to actually open it up to those for whom it was intended. It was a constant worry to President Bryce, who privately wondered many times what to do about that "white elephant." Luckily, in 1911 the Battle Creek Sanitarium leased the building for a five-year period.

By the time that lease ran out the association was no more. It had lasted only two years and accomplished very little. The bill it sponsored in Lansing to substitute mediation procedures for strikes and lockouts got nowhere. Most of the people Bryce and others contacted about the association, whether employer or employee, were skeptical of it, and, in all, less than two dozen branches were ever in operation, most of them in Michigan. The nationwide network of free employment bureaus contemplated for association members never amounted to more than five.

Samuel Gompers happily reported its demise: "C. W. Post has discarded another hobby and purpose in life. . . . The Postum 'Trades and Workers Association' fell because it was not a genuine, natural development meeting an actual need of the working people, but was an artificial, exotic fungus which a mere theorist and experimenter attempted to graft upon industrial institutions. . . . Mr. Post says his plan failed because he was unable to interest workingmen in the proposition. ... It is with pleasure we record Mr. Post's acknowledgment of this fact."

Some newspapers explained that the association had dissolved because it was ahead of its time. In a sense this was true since Post was one of the first to establish such an organization. When company unions became more popular, two years after the association had gone by the boards, Gompers continued to identify them as "Post-type" unions.

In 1914, the year of Post's death, the AFL's political drive to rid the labor movement of the injunction specter came to fruition when Congress passed the Clayton Act. The act said, among other things, that "the labor of a human being is not a commodity or article in commerce," that nothing contained in the antitrust laws was to be construed as prohibiting the existence of labor organizations or restraining its members from "lawfully carrying out the legitimate objectives thereof." Nor were such organizations or members of them to "be held or construed to be illegal combinations or conspiracies in restraint of trade, under the antitrust laws." Gompers was jubilant. He hailed the new law as labor's "Magna Carta."

The advent of World War I brought a period of prosperity to the country. During the war effort, harmony prevailed between government, management, and labor; and open shop efforts died down. Organized labor's ranks grew again, and AFL organizers even made some headway in Battle Creek. But the town would be heard from again in its old role in 1921, when the Supreme Court handed down its decision in *Duplex Co.* vs. *Deering.*

The Duplex story goes back to 1913. At the time only three firms in the country made newspaper presses. One of these, the Duplex Printing Company, was a Battle Creek firm and a stout advocate of the open shop. The other two firms dealt with the International Association of Machinists, (IAM) and had agreed to a higher wage scale and an eight-hour day, but only if their Battle Creek competitor could be persuaded to give the same. This it would not do. Consequently, in August 1913 the fourteen members of the IAM employed at Duplex went out on strike. Since the company's employees numbered some 250, the miniscule walk-out hardly mattered in itself. But the IAM then placed a boycott on Duplex presses. Duplex filed a suit against the union, charging that it was "engaged in a conspiracy to restrain . . . [the company's] interstate trade and commerce . . . contrary to the Sherman Anti-Trust Act." The IAM banked on the Clayton Act as its defense, and the lower courts agreed. The case reached the Supreme Court in 1921, and that body reversed the lower courts and found for the company. The Clayton Act, it said, applied only to the immediate dispute between employer and employee. It did not legalize secondary boycotts, nor did it prevent the use of the injunction in cases involving alleged conspiracies in restraint of trade.

Gompers groaned that labor's rights had been "judicially purloined"; labor's "Magna Carta" was in shreds. The fight was on again. Employers sought and received more injunctions than ever, and the open shop movement flourished as never before.

Post would have smiled. His town had learned its lesson well.

4

CRISIS IN THE COPPER COUNTRY

The American Federation of Labor's policy of organizing primarily along craft lines automatically excluded a large number of the semiskilled and unskilled wage earners in the United States. In an increasingly industrialized society, more and more workers found need for union organizations to represent their interests as well as those of the skilled worker.

Given the hostility toward unionism so characteristic of early twentieth century management, it is not surprising that some of the new organizations that emerged to fill that need were extremely militant. They met offensive with counteroffensive. Moreover, governmental support of the employers' position led to a certain amount of political disillusionment, so that radical ideology also found a home among some groups of workers and was reflected in their new labor organizations.

The tendency toward radicalism and extreme militancy was especially marked among the labor organizations that grew up in the frontier atmosphere of the remote mining and lumber areas of the West. There, employer and employee confronted one another in open hostility. In a typical mining or lumbering settlement the employer owned the town and everything in it, and much of the surrounding countryside as well. He either owned or controlled housing, stores, city officials, newspapers, police, and—if there were such amenities—schools, and at times even the pulpit. He usually had the sympathetic ear of the governor and could count on the use of the militia whenever he desired it. Because the work was physically demanding and dangerous and the settlements isolated and rough, the men who worked in the mines and lumbercamps were usually young, single, independent-minded and tough. In such a setting, disputes over working conditions or wages could, and often did, quickly escalate into miniature wars.

One union that evolved in this charged atmosphere was the Western Federation of Miners. The WFM originated in the Butte, Montana, copper region in 1893, and from the beginning, in contrast to the AFL's craft orientation, it was an industrial union, determined to organize all workers associated with nonferrous metal mining into one union. It made no difference whether they worked above or below the ground, in the mines themselves, or in the mills and smelters. Despite the industrial approach of the WFM, for a short period it did affiliate with the AFL, but it was an uneasy alliance and soon was severed. The AFL policy that employer and employee could live together in mutual respect simply did not apply in the western mining towns, and the Federation's cautious, conservative approach was equally futile there. The AFL in turn was appalled at its maverick affiliate's behavior. While it should be stressed that mine managers were certainly equally guilty, the WFM was involved in some of the most ruthless labor battles in American history. Trainwrecks, dynamiting, bludgeonings, and murders were characteristic. Indeed, some of the WFM's early strikes might well be described as class warfare. When the Industrial Workers of the World (IWW) was formed in 1905, its stated creed was that "the working class and the employing class have nothing in common." Not surprisingly, the WFM was a charter member of the IWW.

In joining the so-called Wobblies, the WFM was associating itself with groups who basically had only one thing in common:

they wanted to create an alternative to the AFL. Some, like the more doctrinaire socialists and anarchists, wanted another vehicle primarily because they thought the AFL was politically too far to the right. Others, like many within the WFM and the reform-minded socialists, were principally concerned with the conservatism of Gompers and his group in their trade union outlook. Still others, like the migrant agricultural workers of the western wheatfields, embraced the IWW as the only labor organization that would offer them a home.

It is perhaps not hard to imagine how the IWW looked to much of the American public, representing, as it did, radical politics, militant unionism, and drifters. By the time the Western Federation of Miners began its drive to organize the copper mines of Michigan's Upper Peninsula, it had long since disassociated itself from the IWW. Indeed, it had cooled down sufficiently so that it was again a member in good standing of the American Federation of Labor. Nevertheless, its own early history and its past association with political radicals and "bums" put it at a distinct disadvantage when it confronted the mine managers of Michigan's Copper Country in the summer of 1913. And in one respect the encounter recalled the old days: the WFM strike in Michigan's copper region was the bloodiest the state had experienced.

The strike began in July 1913 and the last remnants of the strikers did not concede defeat until almost ten months later, in April 1914. In the interim the conflict shook the Copper Country as never before.

The Copper Country embraces Keewenaw, Houghton, and Ontonagon counties in the Upper Peninsula. Prehistoric Indians had mined the metal long before the days of Columbus, but when the white man came to that area, these early miners had long since vanished. Only their long-abandoned diggings remained. Stories about the copper of the area drifted back to the kings of France and England all through the colonial period, but the region was, in Patrick Henry's words, "beyond the most distant wilderness and remote as the moon," and few men cared to venture there.

Soon after Michigan became a state in 1837, interest in the area was renewed. Congress had assigned the Upper Peninsula to the new state to soothe ruffled feelings at the loss of the Toledo area to Ohio, and a few Michiganders soon showed an interest in finding out just what had been acquired. A young physician, Douglass Houghton, was dubbed "state geologist" by the legislature and told to go and see. The report of his findings triggered the first major mining boom in the United States. Five years before the forty-niners rushed to California, men like them swarmed to Michigan's Copper Country. Michigan became the leading copper producer in the country and remained so until the 1880s when the Montana mines came into production.

Initially, mining activity centered in Keewenaw and Ontonagon counties, but by the early 1900s the major mines were clustered in Houghton County. Calumet & Hecla Mining Company, accounting for over 60 percent of the district's output, was the dominant employer and the leading policy maker.

The 1913–14 strike was not the first among the copper miners of Michigan, but earlier ones had usually been local, often spontaneous, and short-lived. Their purpose had generally been to raise wages, and the companies had often acceded to the demands made, at least partially, although the strike leaders usually found themselves out of a job. No union had ever made much real headway—at least not for long.

A major reason for the companies' overall success in keeping unions out was the very liberal benefits policies they had instituted. As far back as 1877, Calumet & Hecla had set up a sickness, death, and disability fund, and other companies soon followed suit. The companies provided good housing at very nominal rents, built free libraries, gymnasiums, and public baths. They built churches, provided schools that used the most modern educational methods, paved the streets, and even collected the garbage free of charge. Some companies maintained stores but, contrary to the stereotype of the gouging "company store," these charged reasonable prices and served to keep charges down at the privately owned stores. No worker was required to trade at a company store, again in contrast to practices established in other mining towns. If an employee or a member of his family was ill, he was treated by company doctors or went to a company hospital. Medicines were also provided free. Space was set aside for social and athletic clubs, and Calumet & Hecla went so far as to supply uniforms, instruments, music, and the conductor for what was said to be one of the best brass bands in the country. When the bandsmen rehearsed or went on concert tour, they continued to receive their regular wages.

The Michigan copper mining communities, then, were a far cry from the raw, isolated towns of the western mining areas. Under the paternal eyes of the Michigan mine managers, comfortable communities had been developed where one could raise a family and live what was, for those times, a pleasant and varied life.

In the early decades of the twentieth century, many of the men working in the copper mines were foreign-born—Finns, Croatians, Hungarians, Italians, Poles—often newly arrived and barely able to speak English. While the companies attempted to make the transition easier by stocking the libraries with foreign-language newspapers, magazines, and books, the fact that there was such a large foreign element added to the animosities that played an important role during the course of the 1913–14 strike. The nation was then undergoing a period of antiforeign feeling, directed particularly against the wave of immigrants coming in from central and eastern Europe. Some Americans contended that the newcomers were, somehow, a lower order of humanity. Others, refuting that, asserted that it was not that the countries they came from produced an inferior product, on the whole, but rather that the United States had become those countries' dumping ground for undesirables. This attitude was reflected in the Copper Country. For example, a high official in the National Guard, writing from the scene to Michigan's governor during the course of the strike, admitted that he thought the mine managers acted like kings in their districts, and that such behavior was clearly un-American. Still, he came to the managers' defense: "they are not dealing with American citizens. I am satisfied a large proportion of the present population has to be ruled and provided for as the mine operators rule and provide for them. They are not capable of self-government nor of adopting methods to better themselves." The fault, then, so far as he was concerned, lay not with management, but with the kind of labor it had to deal with.

Tension heightened because the English-speaking workers—Cornish, Irish, or native-born—usually held the better jobs in the mines, including that of mine foreman. The foremen could, and apparently often did, tyrannize the men under them. They considered the immigrants "dumb foreigners" and treated them that way. In theory the men could have gone over the foreman's head to complain; in practice this did not happen. Language was often a barrier, and even where it was not, all too often the managers automatically sided with their supervisory personnel. Those who complained ultimately found themselves out of job; and it is not surprising that this often caused resentment among the men and added to the friction between nationality groups.

It was not simply the "inferior" foreigner who worried the American public in those years but also the "dangerous" newcomer, the one bringing in radical ideologies—socialism, anarcho-syndicalism, and communism. This group of foreigners, many believed, would put wrong ideas into the heads of their more gullible countrymen.

During the early years of the twentieth century the Socialist Party achieved its greatest political success in the United States. In 1912 there were 56 Socialist mayors in office throughout the U. S., and Eugene Debs had polled almost 6 percent of the popular vote for president in the fall election. While the Socialists made no headway in Copper Country politics, a local Socialist club, composed of members of the Finnish community, did exist. The specter of radicalism, then, was not entirely absent in the area. Fear that the community might become infiltrated with radical ideas grew once the WFM entered the district. Given the union's past reputation, it was easy to characterize WFM organizers as "outside agitators" who would lead the impressionable newcomers astray. Calumet & Hecla's manager reported to a U. S. Senate committee that the foreigners working for his concern "are industrious loyal men; but they do not know our language or our customs, our laws, nor our ideals. They have been influenced by the Western Federation of Miner's organizers and hired men who have been here in some cases for years. Constant dropping will wear a stone." The companies kept maintaining throughout the strike that the whole affair was attributable solely to the work of socialist-minded outsiders determined to stir up trouble.

Actually, political ideology played no part in the union's organizing drive in the Copper Country. The WFM initially made wages their primary issue. Until the turn of the century wages had been good in the region. By the early 1900s, however, the Michigan copper veins were becoming increasingly costly to mine. The metal nearer the surface was exhausted, and shafts had gone deeper and deeper. The copper concentration in the newer veins was lower. At the same time, more and more western mines, which contained a copper relatively inexpensive to extract and process, opened up. In the face of this competition, wages paid by the Michigan companies had begun to lag. By 1909 the Montana worker averaged $3.87 a day, while his Michigan counterpart received only $2.36. The Michigan miner also worked about an hour longer a day for this wage.

Even with this issue the WFM drive made little headway for the first few years. Perhaps the Michigan miners viewed the wage differential as compensation for the frontier conditions in the western towns, and the cost of living in the west was said to be much higher.

Resentment simmered, nevertheless. The paternalism of the Michigan companies, while it offered many advantages, also meant, as one man put it, "your home was heated with coal brought on company boats, you washed in water from company pumps, had your dinner under company-made electric lights." One man who had worked for Calumet & Hecla for years reported that "the Company always made him think of that time-honored advertisement of some forgotten furniture concern: 'We Stand Behind Every One of Our Beds.'"

A U. S. Department of Labor investigator visiting the area during the strike said it differently, but it amounted to the same thing: "The impression I received from the trip was that the condition of benevolent feudalism exists in the copper country. It would be unfair to the Calumet & Hecla and to the people generally to say that the conditions are bad, so far as housing and working conditions are concerned. On the contrary, I think the company has done a great deal of welfare work for its employees and to that extent is deserving credit. Only one thing appeared to be lacking and that is the right of the workers to be free men in every sense of the word."

Beyond this, all of the companies instituted extensive cost-cutting campaigns in the years just prior to the strike. This not only affected wages, but involved a push for increased productivity and the introduction of labor-saving devices. As one observer noted, "the mine owners have a spirit of wishing to do something for the welfare of their men, but in recent years they have not let that spirit interfere with their cutting of cost and paying of dividends."

The introduction of a new labor-saving device, the so-called one-man drill, was instrumental in triggering interest in joining the union. The miners had been using a drill that required two men, which not only afforded companionship but also a certain amount of protection in case of emergency, which the man working alone would not have. Many miners considered the new drill dangerous and soon nicknamed it "the widow-maker." Moreover, the one-man drill was heavy and cumbersome to assemble and had to be put up and torn down almost every day. While the companies did not prohibit two men from working together in doing that part of the drilling operation, neither had they established any clear rules about it. And the new machine was obviously a threat to employment, since one man could now do what two had done before.

Not all the miners agreed that the new drill was an evil, and ample evidence was presented during the strike indicating that a man working the one-man drill on piece rate earned more than one using the old machine. Nonetheless, many miners disliked the new machine and protested to the companies against its introduction. Their protests fell on deaf ears. It may have been the companies' attitude toward the complaints as much as the new drill itself that caused discontent. Whatever the cause, WFM ranks grew.

By the early summer of 1913 the Western Federation had five locals in the area: three in Houghton County, one in Keewenaw, and the other in Ontonagon. Organization was heaviest among the underground miners and the "trammers," the men who pushed the loaded tramcars to the lifts. Only a small number of surface employees ever joined the union. Perhaps one half of all underground men in the Copper Country were organized by the time the strike began. Underground men at Calumet & Hecla were least organized. That company consistently paid the highest wages in the area and had recently raised them even further. It offered the best benefits program, even a retirement pension plan. In addition, its local labor force, above and below the ground, contained a majority of the English-speaking workers of the Copper Country. Overall, this group had proved harder to organize. All of these things set the majority of the Calumet & Hecla employees off from the rest, which made the key company in the district the weakest in terms of union membership.

The Calumet & Hecla trammers were the one exception. There were, for one, more non-English-speaking among this group. Also, as "tramming" was always done by young men, because it was physically exhausting work, the trammers were often unmarried, more likely to drift from job to job, and thus less interested in an employer's benefits program. While the Calumet & Hecla trammer's wage was $.35 a day higher than that of trammers at other Copper Country mines, it was still a low daily wage—$2.75. Of all the mineworkers, the trammers as a group had been most affected by the production speed-up, since they ultimately had to move the increased amount of ore out of the mines. The one-man drill also constituted an issue among the trammers. All of them hoped to become miners, and if the new drill threatened the employment of the present miners, the trammers' chances for advancement were very slim indeed.

The Western Federation officials were heartened by their gains in membership in the Copper Country and felt that perhaps by April 1914 their organizational drive would be successful enough to allow them to confront the companies. In the interim, they urged caution. The local rank and file felt otherwise. They were restless. They kept goading the local leadership and grumbled that they were dragging their feet. Despite national headquarters' qualms the discontented membership forced the local leaders to disregard the national's advice. The local leaders, under pressure, "jumped the gun."

In mid-July 1913 the local leaders sent an identical letter to each company's top officials, asking for a meeting to discuss "possibilities of shortening the working day, raising wages, and making some changes in the working conditions." The letter also asked for a reply no later than July 21. Failure to reply, it went on, would be taken as proof that the companies were unwilling to meet and settle matters peaceably. One company sent the letter back to union headquarters unopened; none replied. In public statements, however, they made clear that they would close the mines rather than meet with the union. Despite this, the union waited until the July 21 deadline had passed. It then called a membership meeting for the next day, where the strike was set for the following day, July 23. The next morning, as miners came off the night shift, strikers passed out leaflets announcing the strike, and a picket line surrounded each entrance. Nonunion men attempting to go to work were persuaded, sometimes forcibly, to change their minds. After an initial clash, in which sixteen men, all nonunion, were hospitalized, the companies decided not to try to operate. By the end of the next day, all twenty-one active mines in the Copper Country were down and some 16,000 employees were idle.

The strike hardly took the companies by surprise. Rumors of a strike had circulated since the first of the year, and the companies had prepared themselves. Even before the strike the sheriff of Houghton County had sworn in extra deputies, and on the day it broke out loyal company employees were also added to the force. Before the strike was over the sheriff had deputized about 1700 men.

Strangely enough, when that first morning's violence took place, the sheriff and his deputies did nothing to stop it. Yet early the next morning the sheriff frantically telegraphed Michigan's governor urging him to send 2000 National Guardsmen to the district because conditions were out of control. His telegram talked of "armed rioters" destroying property and threatening lives and predicted that the situation would get worse without outside help. The governor responded immediately by dispatching nearby companies. Then, after a continued bombardment of telegrams from the sheriff and others, he sent in the whole Michigan contingent of the Guard: 211 officers and 2,354 enlisted men. Most of the guardsmen were stationed

around the mines of Houghton County. It was only with diffi-
culty that the sheriff at Keewenaw County was persuaded to let
them protect one mine in his area. The population of
Keewenaw County was composed almost wholly of mineworkers
and their families, in contrast to Houghton County, which
contained a large commercial, professional, and managerial element. Thus officials in Keewenaw County, including the sheriff,
were more sympathetic to the striking miners than were those
of Houghton County.

At the time the Guard was dispatched to the Copper Country,
Pancho Villa, the Mexican revolutionary, was causing concern
to U. S. policy makers, and a Houghton newspaper reported that
Guard officers were enthusiastic about the opportunity to send
troops to the Copper Country: "the invaluable training received . . . will be of inestimable service in case hostilities break

An encampment of Michigan National Guardsmen at Calumet in 1913
during the copper mine strike

out between the United States and Mexico. It is probable that in event of war being declared the Michigan troops would be the first to be sent to the front because of their services here, which is exactly the same as they would receive in the field in time of actual warfare."

With the approval of the Houghton County board of supervisors, which was composed largely of mine managers, the county sheriff had contacted James Waddell two weeks before the strike began. Waddell headed the Mahon-Waddell Corporation, which was billed as "an organization that specializes in labor disputes." Waddell himself was on the scene from the beginning, and two days after the strike began the county added 52 Waddell men to the payroll to assist the sheriff and his men and train his new deputies.

Waddell's gunmen had such an unsavory reputation that the manager of Calumet & Hecla declared that he would rather hire "Lefty Louie" or "Gyp the Blood" than put them on his company payroll. Instead, he and other top company officials used Pinkertons as personal body guards, and during the course of the strike hired guards from another agency to protect company property. (The manager did admit that the latter weren't "kid-glove fellows" either.) Calumet & Hecla's manager drew a rather fine line in any event: as the controlling voice on the Houghton County board of supervisors he apparently saw nothing wrong with adding Waddell's men to the county payroll. And they did not come cheap—through the end of August their salaries and expenses alone cost the county $10,000. Other mining companies also added private guards to their own staffs, usually Waddell agents.

This was marvelous publicity for James Waddell, and he made the most of it. In the course of the strike he sent out a circular to a number of large corporations pointing with pride to his agency's activities in the Upper Peninsula: "We ask you to watch the progress of the present strike, because we know it will be a triumph for law and order, a triumph for the mine owners, and will furnish still another evidence of the success we have always met in breaking strikes."

Following the initial violence, there was relative calm in the Copper Country for a time. The companies initially made no attempt to reopen, paid the strikers what was due them on payday, and permitted them to continue to live in company housing and use company medical facilities. On the other side, the union was careful then, as throughout the strike, not to damage company property. One thing the union did was agree to permit union men to operate the pumps to keep the mines from flooding. Picketing was peaceful, and union parades were orderly. Some of the idled miners left the area to find other work, and those remaining subsisted on strike benefits paid by the WFM and from donations from a number of AFL unions. Chief among the latter was the United Mine Workers. Men from that union, like John L. Lewis and John Mitchell, visited the area and added moral support as well.

With everything so quiet, the newspapermen who had been assigned to cover the strike began to drift away. The Michigan taxpayers noted the calm and started questioning the need for so many troops in the area, which were costing the state $12,500 a day. The governor prodded the sheriff to organize his own forces to handle matters, and by the second week in August the governor began gradually to whittle down the size of the guard forces.

In the first week of August the mine managers announced that they would reopen soon and appealed to their employees to come back to work. A number of nonunion men agreed to do so, provided they were protected. Calumet & Hecla was particularly successful in its back-to-work drive, although a number of other mines also began limited operations during the month. The union responded by resuming large-scale picketing around the mines. Despite WFM warnings against the use of violence, some minor outbreaks took place between strikers and nonunion men. A few incidents between strikers and guardsmen also occurred, but most were not serious. In his communications to the commanding officer of the Guard, the governor constantly stressed that the troops were there only to protect life and property: "Are we agreed that the National Guard cannot under any circumstances take sides even directly or indirectly in the settlement of this industrial dispute?" "I am sure that you and your soldiers will do your level best to be as nearly neutral as it is possible to be all the way through the strike." Overall, the guardsmen heeded his message.

The serious troubles arose with the Waddell-trained deputies and particularly with the Waddell men themselves. The Waddell men had been brought in to break the strike and were ready to provoke riots and disorder to accomplish that purpose. As one of them later testified, "The understanding with the strike-breaking agency [Mahon-Waddell] is this: If there is enough excitement and riot going on, we don't need to be creating it. If there is not any we ought to create some."

Legally the sheriff could not deputize the Waddell men since they were not local residents. He permitted them, however, to act as if they had been deputized. They were such an unsavory lot that even prominent citizens in the area, who had little sympathy for the strike, began to protest that it was dangerous to have the Waddell agents around.

Their fears proved justified. The worst incident took place the evening of August 14, in the small village of Seeberville. A striker, walking home to his boardinghouse, took a traditional shortcut across property owned by the Copper Range Consolidated Mining Company. One of the deputies stopped him, but he protested that he always came that way and continued. Shortly after he reached his boardinghouse, the deputy, accompanied by another and four Waddell men, arrived to arrest him on the charge of intimidating a law officer. The striker and some other lodgers were outside when the six men arrived but, after a scuffle, ran into the house. The deputies and Waddell men then began shooting into the house, firing indiscriminately through doors and windows until their revolvers were empty. Two men in the house were killed, two others seriously wounded, and a six-month old baby also hurt. After the six men had emptied their guns, witnesses saw them collect tin cans, rocks, and bottles and strew them around the house, presumably to make it look as if the boarders had been pelting them with objects. The six also told investigators that the first shot had been fired from within the house. When the Houghton County sheriff arrived on the scene, he accepted their story. But since no gun could be found in the boardinghouse, and witnesses insisted that no shots had been fired from inside, the sheriff was eventually forced to yield to public pressure and arrest the six men. In time, four were indicted for manslaughter. A fifth, a Waddell agent, jumped bail prior to the trial, and the remaining man—the deputy who had originally challenged the striker—was found innocent.

These six men, and a deputy who shot a fourteen-year-old girl marching in a picket parade on September 2, were the only nonstrikers arrested during the course of the strike. In contrast, during the same period over 600 strikers were arrested, usually on the charge of intimidating an officer or inciting a riot. Another 500 were arrested for violating an injunction against picketing and parading that the companies succeeded in securing in September.

An investigator sent in by the U.S. Bureau of Labor Statistics commented on the difference in treatment: "When the strikers mistreated the men that went to work during the strike they were arrested and fined, imprisoned or bound over. But when peace officers, deputy sheriffs, soldiers or Waddell men engaged in conflicts with the strikers and the officers were the aggressors in beating or riding down the strikers, there was no one to arrest the officers." In the end, indictments against the strikers were few, but the damage had been done.

Meanwhile, companies were reopening mines and adding additional guards, often with labor from outside the region to supplement their work force. The trammers, particularly, were not coming back, even to Calumet & Hecla. Initially the men being brought in were not told of the strike in the Copper Country. Consequently, once the new arrivals saw the soldiers and the picketers, company guards had to be used to keep them in, as well as to keep the strikers out. Some of them managed to escape, however, and told of their captivity. This brought protests from their consular agents (the men were generally newly arrived immigrants) and adverse publicity to the companies. Thereafter, the mine managers tried to make sure that the men they hired knew exactly what the situation was.

As it became clear that the companies had no intention of bargaining with the union, the Western Federation sought outside help. Officials appealed to the governor to step in. The governor had very little power to act. Just two years before the state legislature had specifically repealed an act that would have required a state investigation and a full public report in case of refusal to accept outside mediators. Nevertheless, the chief executive sent in investigators and, toward the end of the strike, came to the area himself. He prodded and cajoled the companies until finally, in exasperation, he telegraphed them, "Sooner or later in this country the Golden Rule has got to come into use. In other words, I believe that business must recognize another end than that of making money. It must recognize the higher end of occasionally rendering service to all." This moved the companies not at all, and there was nothing further he could do.

The union had high hopes when the U. S. Department of Labor sent in an investigator in mid-September 1913; but he had no more success with the employers than did the governor. They would not meet with the WFM, directly or indirectly.

The companies saw no purpose in mediation, although this was urged on them a number of times by many outsiders. The Calumet & Hecla manager summed up their attitude: "This is my pocketbook. I won't arbitrate with you as to whose pocketbook this is. It is mine. Now it would be foolish to arbitrate that question; I have decided it in my own mind ... These men [the strikers] can find employment elsewhere. If they do not want to subscribe to the conditions that we impose, they are perfectly free to go to other places."

As the lines between employers and strikers hardened, more violence broke out. Attempts were made to dynamite or derail trains bringing in new workers, but the engineers always seemed to know where to stop the trains to avoid an accident. (How they knew was never revealed.) Strikers did succeed in damaging the railroad cars by throwing stones at the windows or shooting at them. Before guards were put on the trains, strikers also assaulted men being brought in, and a number of them had to be hospitalized.

In late November shots were fired into a boardinghouse where a number of Lithuanians who had returned to work were living. The WFM claimed that this was the work of a few malcontents and, luckily, no one was hurt. But the act hurt the union's cause with the community.

On December 1 the companies instituted an eight-hour work-day and raised wages. They also announced the establishment of a grievance procedure. The mine managers denied that these moves were in any way connected with the strike, but it seems clear that, in fact, the steps were taken to undermine the union. Of the original demands made by the Western Federation, the companies' action left only two outstanding: two men on the one-man drill and recognition of the Western Federation of Miners. The strikers were ready to drop the drill question, so that left the issue of union recognition as the only one the men were really holding out for. The strikers' ranks began to dwindle.

The union's image was further tarnished when, on December 7, another shooting took place, this time into a boardinghouse filled with men who either had returned to work or were known to be planning to. Three men were killed. Whatever sympathy was left toward the strikers now vanished. The murders so infuriated the returned miners that some 4300 petitioned Calumet & Hecla not to take back any members of the union and, furthermore, suggested that the company evict them from their homes. The company manager was delighted with the first request since he had already stipulated that the company would not reeemploy anyone who did not give up his membership in the WFM. As to the second, however, he refused. It was not "the proper thing . . . to do during the winter months."

The shooting also set the community in motion. A "citizens alliance," formed in November but quiescent until the shooting, now went into action. Together with the Houghton County sheriff's men, alliance members systematically searched every striker's home, every union hall, and the men themselves for firearms. They ran one organizer out of the district and threatened others. Calls went out to the governor to declare martial law and send back the Guard. This time the governor refused; it was a local matter and should be handled locally.

The WFM finally succeeded in obtaining a restraining order against the citizens alliance, which put a damper on its activities. Union officials also pleaded with the strikers to remain peaceful. It looked as if order had been restored, at least over the upcoming Christmas holidays.

On the afternoon of December 24, the WFM women's auxiliary was holding a Christmas party for the children on the second floor of a hall in Calumet. Some 700 to 800 people were at the affair. Just as it was about to break up, someone yelled "fire!" There was a stampede to the stairwell, pushing, shoving, screaming, and panic. People stumbled and fell, and the crowd behind simply trampled over them. When it was over, sixty-two children and eleven adults were found dead. There had, in fact, been no fire, and the coroner's jury and a later Congressional investigating committee failed to pin down who had cried out, or why.

The tragedy aroused sympathy for the families throughout the district. Clothing, food, and between $25,000 and $30,000 were collected for their relief. On the day after Christmas, relief committees visited the strikers' homes to distribute what had been collected. At some homes they were told, "Yes, we need help; we want help; but we dare not take it. We are told we must not take it." At others they were simply turned away.

These refusals were blamed on the Western Federation. Right after the event WFM President William Moyer had issued a statement about the disaster. Among other things, he stated that he had heard a number of stories about how the fire scare had started, one that the person who had shouted "fire!" was wearing a citizens alliance button. He also said he knew about the relief committees, but went on to say, "the Western Federation of Miners will bury its own dead and the American labor movement will take care of the relatives of the deceased." These remarks infuriated the citizens alliance. As one member later said, "You can imagine the feeling in the county, or rather you can not imagine it. It is impossible to describe or to imagine it, unless you have felt it yourself." Moyer later said that his statement that the union would take care of its own was meant to answer questions raised by the strikers and their families, who were reluctant to take outside help unless they had to. But the alliance men interpreted it as an order to the strikers to refuse help. To them, the Western Federation had split the community apart.

A delegation from the alliance came to see Moyer at his hotel room in Hancock and tried to persuade him to tell the families to take what had been collected. He refused. They then asked him at least to do something about the rumors that the alliance had deliberately planned the disaster. Moyer replied that he would call the various local headquarters and ask them not to talk about who was responsible, one way or another. That was as far as he would go.

The members of the delegation were unhappy with Moyer's reaction but left. There is some discrepancy between their version and Moyer's as to whether or not they threatened him as they were leaving. In any event, right after they left there was a knock on the door and a gang of armed men, wearing alliance buttons, seized Moyer and began beating him. In the scuffle he was also shot. Then he and another union official were dragged out of the hotel and to the railroad station a mile away. They were then thrown into the train and the conductor was told that they were to be sent to Chicago, and that the sheriff of Houghton County would pay their fares. When the two men reached Chicago, Moyer had to be hospitalized for ten days.

The Christmas Eve tragedy and Moyer shooting brought on another U. S. Department of Labor investigation and the governor's visit to the area. It also triggered a lengthy congressional investigation, which began hearings in February 1914. The committee met in Hancock for over a month to take testimony and then moved on to Chicago. It finally wound up its hearings in Washington in late March. The committee heard lengthy testimony concerning the miners' grievances, and not just those that the union had put forward earlier. Miners spoke of the unsanitary working conditions, the poor ventilation in the mines, and similar topics. But by this time, the Western Federation's position in the Copper Country had so deteriorated that union leaders had very little hope that the congressional investigation would do any good. They told the committee that all they were now asking of the employers was that they take back the remaining strikers despite their union membership. This astounded the congressmen. As one committee member said: "Do I understand that you want to have the Committee make a report in which they would make no criticism of these alleged man-killing machines, unsanitary conditions in the mines, as to which there has been evidence introduced here that they are unhealthful; that a man could not live more than five or six or seven years? All those things to be relegated to the rear as mere incidents?" Their astonishment was not lessened when the union representative answered that he thought the companies had shown an honest desire to right the wrongs, that they would eventually be taken care of, and that only the "greater, broader question" of union membership still need settling.

The employers' attitude was less puzzling to the committee. From the beginning they had wanted the Western Federation of Miners eliminated from the Copper Country, and they had not changed their minds: "The Western Federation of Miners, by reason of history, its record, and its record in this district as well as elsewhere, is persona non grata to the operators and will continue to be so."

About the time the hearings drew to a close in Washington, the union announced a cutback of strike benefits. Some two weeks later the United Mine Workers—the last support left—told the WFM it could no longer send funds. It was having troubles of its own in Ohio.

It was clear that the strike was in effect over. The companies announced that they would take back the men as soon as there were openings, and that they would let them stay in their homes and provide help until then. They made only one provision: that the men renounce their union membership.

On Sunday, April 12, 1914, the few remaining strikers took a vote and by a 3–1 margin decided to end the strike. The next morning they tore up their union cards and went to the mine employment offices. Unionism was dead in the Copper Country and would be for another quarter of a century.

Postscript

The primary reason for the loss of the strike in the Copper Country was simply that it was called too soon. Yet the WFM's past history of extreme militance and political radicalism was also a decided handicap, which continued to plague the organization for years. While the union's leadership was committed to a more conservative course at the time of the copper strike, a vocal minority among its members had never reconciled themselves to that attitude. The issue of political radicalism arose again soon after the Michigan strike ended. The conflict centered within the WFM's largest and richest local, in Butte, Montana. When the smoke of battle cleared, Butte, a WFM stronghold for twenty years, was an open shop mining town. This was a staggering blow to the union.

The outbreak of World War I brought renewed prosperity to the copper mining industry, just as it sparked the American economy as a whole. The war years also represented an epoch in which much of the American labor movement enjoyed a respite from employer hostility and governmental interference. This, however, did not apply to that segment of organized labor that had become identified in the public mind with radical ideology. The war put a premium on 100 percent loyalty to the country and its institutions, and at times a ruthless campaign was waged against any person or organization that did not appear to conform to that pattern.

In an effort to disassociate itself from the taint of radicalism the WFM changed its name to the International Union of Mine, Mill and Smelter Workers in 1916. As such, the much weakened organization survived for a number of years, primarily in the isolated western mining towns. In the 1930s, as a CIO affiliate, it entered a few localities in the East, including Michigan's Copper Country; but it never wholly freed itself of its past. After World War II the union was expelled from the CIO on charges of Communist infiltration, and the organization and its leaders were harassed for over a decade by the U. S. Department of Justice on related grounds.

In its January 18, 1967, issue *The New York Times* reported the passing of "one of the few remaining old-line radical labor groups" in the country. The day before, the remaining members of the International Union of Mine, Mill and Smelter Workers had voted to merge with the United Steelworkers of America.

The old Western Federation of Miners had finally entered the mainstream of American labor history.

5

LABOR MARCHES SITTING DOWN

It was no accident that Michigan became the home of the automotive industry. As far back as 1863, the state's iron deposits, coupled with the ease and low cost of transport on the Great Lakes, had been major factors in locating the nation's first Bessemer steel plant in Wyandotte. By the 1880s and 1890s these same assets and Michigan's lumber and copper supplies had made Detroit a center for machine and metalworking shops. They also accounted for the fact that the state was an important center for the bicycle and carriage industries. In the years just previous to the development of the automobile the bicycle was for a time "all the rage" with the American public. But the fad soon passed, and as the bicycle became less fashionable production figures took a dip. Moreover, by the mid-1880s Michigan's lumber was running thin, and carriage makers were beginning to move out of the state to follow the wood supply. Thus just as the automobile was being developed, Michigan had a ready supply of workers long familiar with making and assembling wheels, gears and machines who were looking for jobs, and a host of parts manufacturers eager to supply a new market.

The state's first approximation of a horseless carriage was built by the Olds Motor Works in Lansing in 1887. It was not a phenomenal success. According to one description, it was "a very crude affair and looked more like a traction engine than an automobile. ... This carriage was a steam machine with an upright boiler using coal for fuel and was run but very little and will be remembered by the older citizens of its home town as the laughing stock of the community." The Olds people soon abandoned the coal-burning monster and built a lighter, smaller vehicle with a gas-burning steam engine. That model was sold to a medicine company that shipped it to London as an advertising gimmick, and it was not heard from again. By the closing years of the nineteenth century, the company had changed over to the internal combustion engine and had succeeded in producing a practical machine. In 1899 the firm built the first factory in the United States specifically designed to manufacture automobiles. It was located in Detroit and could turn out eighteen cars a day.

Initially, the automobile was a hobby that only the well-to-do could indulge. The price was too high for a mass market. Cars usually sold for from $1000 to $2000, at a time when the average annual wage was between $500 and $600. And full payment was expected on delivery. Even so, interest was great enough so that Olds and his growing list of competitors kept expanding their plants and adding to their labor force in an effort to keep up with the demand. For example, in 1905, the year Michigan took the lead in auto manufacturing in the country, the state's firms employed just over 4000 people and turned out 28,830 vehicles. Only five years later their production had increased to 315,000 units, and the number of employees had risen to just under 40,000. The latter figure does not include those working in automobile accessories shops—perhaps another 10,000.

The succeeding decades saw changes in car design and production methods—the moving assembly line was introduced at Ford's Highland Park plant in 1913—as well as the introduction of installment buying, which transformed the motor car from a luxury item to a product available to the mass market. By 1929 the auto industry, in terms of value of product, was the leading manufacturing industry in the country. Well over 5 million cars, trucks, and buses were turned out that year by nearly 448,000 autoworkers. Michigan, particularly the Detroit area, accounted for about half of both figures.

When the industry was new, a number of small manufacturers had entered the field. In 1910 representatives of the Michigan Department of Labor canvassed almost fifty automakers in the state and found that some plants produced as few as 100 to 300 vehicles a year, while the largest producer, the Ford Motor Company, had an annual volume of 67,500. By 1929 this pattern had changed considerably. In the interim, most of the small companies had either gone under or been swallowed up by the larger firms and three companies—Ford, General Motors, and Chrysler—clearly dominated the industry. Among them, the three accounted for over three quarters of all cars produced that year. Ford was still the largest of the three in 1929, although in 1931 GM took over the lead and, since then, has never relinquished it.

Unions played a negligible role in the industry until the New Deal period. One AFL affiliate, the Carriage, Wagon and Automobile Workers (CWAW), succeeded in organizing workers in the small auto body and supply shops in the years prior to and during World War I. However, that union constantly had to contend with jurisdictional claims made by the older craft unions. The painters, metal polishers, and upholsterers unions jealously guarded their own interests among the skilled workers in the industry, although, in fact, they organized very few of them. Friction over this issue led to the expulsion of the CWAW from the AFL in 1918. After the ouster, the CWAW was reorganized as the United Automobile, Aircraft and Vehicle Workers and continued to grow for another two years. At its peak, in 1920, the auto union claimed some 45,400 members. If this figure is accurate, it means that the organization had enrolled about 11 percent of the workers in the industry. Even then, however, it had made no real inroads into the large manufacturing concerns. The larger firms could combat organizational pressure more effectively than could the small shops.

In addition, wages were higher and working conditions generally better in the larger organizations so that workers were less interested in unionizing.

Overall, the auto industry was a high wage industry. In 1910, for example, an auto worker in Michigan averaged $2.78 a day while the statewide rate for men in factory work generally was $2.19. In January 1914, to the dismay of his competitors, Henry Ford announced his $5-a-day policy. The resultant stampede to his employment office was formidable, and other companies soon found it advisable to raise wage rates in line with Ford's to keep their labor force intact. As a result, a steady stream of would-be auto workers descended upon the automobile manufacturing centers. Employers soon came to see the line at the employment door as the best means of assuring steady production.

After 1920 the auto union rapidly disintegrated. The organization's decline was due in part to the 1920–21 postwar recession and the disappointing results of strike action taken during the period. An additional factor was the resurgence of the open shop drive by employer groups throughout the country. Open shop advocates now labeled their movement the "American Plan," with the obvious connotation that to advocate the organization of labor—and particularly the closed shop—was "un-American." Unionism was often declared to be synonymous with socialism and Bolshevism. One spokesman for the National Association of Manufacturers went even further and implied that to be for the closed shop was to be against the Ten Commandments: "When the people of this enlightened country surrender to the absurdity of the argument for the so-called closed shop and accept it as an established institution, they will owe it to the devil to repudiate the Decalogue and repeal the Constitution of the United States."

Auto manufacturers gave their wholehearted support to the open shop drive and, as a corollary to it, vigorously embraced "welfare capitalism." The auto companies added such traditional "industrial betterment" features as death benefit plans, emergency medical facilities, recreational facilities, and social clubs. A less pleasant feature was the increasing use of "labor spies" to stamp out organizational efforts before they could make headway. The companies also continued to advertise their high wage policies, although the advertisement sometimes exceeded reality. Ford, for example, gave no general wage increase between 1919 and 1929. Moreover, toward the end of that decade the company was rehiring, after model changeover layoffs, at beginners' rates rather than at the rate the particular employee had received before layoff.

Throughout the 1920s the manufacturers' efforts to keep unions out proved extremely effective. Indeed, the auto industry generally, and Detroit especially, served as shining examples for open shop advocates everywhere. The industry was booming, and its flourishing condition was commonly attributed to the fact that the auto manufacturers adhered closely to open shop principles. The fact that during the prosperous 1920s Americans bought more cars than ever was not permitted to muddle the argument.

Employers were not alone, however, in hindering unionization in the auto plants of the 1920s. Part of the blame rests squarely on the AFL, still the dominant labor organization in the country and the only one with sufficient resources to accomplish a job of such magnitude. The Federation's craft orientation was simply not suited to a mass production industry, but the bulk of the organization's leaders were unwilling or unable to adjust themselves to the fact. As early as 1920, only about 1 percent of the total labor force in the auto industry could be classified among the highly skilled. In 1922 Henry Ford estimated that 85 percent of his labor force required less than two weeks of training, and, of those, 43 percent needed only a day to be broken in. Yet the few AFL leaders who recognized industrywide organization as the only feasible way of dealing with the problem were consistently howled down by the leaders of the craft unions who feared encroachment upon their own jurisdictions.

The most serious attempt made by the Federation to organize auto came in 1926, just after that body's annual convention. The meeting had been held in Detroit, and the delegates had seen at first hand the extent of the Motor City's commitment to the open shop principle. Delegates' offers to address church congregations while they were in town brought an immediate request from members of the Detroit Board of Commerce for equal time. An invitation issued to AFL President William Green to talk to a YMCA group in Detroit had to be hastily withdrawn because the YMCA's board of directors reacted so adversely to the idea.

The AFL convention delegates authorized the Federation to undertake a massive organizational drive in the auto industry "at the earliest possible date." Federation efforts foundered, however, primarily on the question of the skilled auto workers. The craft unions insisted that those with skills be parceled out among the appropriate old-line unions, but for the most part they were quite unwilling to have anything whatever to do with the semiskilled or unskilled workers that signed up. Yet the crafts were wary of any suggestion that the less skilled have an organization of their own.

Detroit police breaking up a demonstration of unemployed in 1930

The drive also suffered because the increasingly cautious Federation leadership also believed it had to have prior consent from the employers before organization could be attempted in the auto plants. AFL President Green made it quite clear that the Federation had no wish "to make war on industry." Instead, unionization was to be accomplished in a spirit of union-management cooperation. Somehow the manufacturers' permission to enter the plants was not forthcoming. The 1926 campaign, then, was doomed at the outset. The Federation made no further move to organize auto until the 1930s, after the onset of the Great Depression.

The Depression that began in 1929 was particularly devastating to the auto industry. The hard-hit American consumer could readily put off the purchase of a new car. As a consequence, production dropped from over 5 million cars in 1929 to just over 1.3 million three years later. The industry cut its active labor force almost in half during the same years, and most of those fortunate enough to have jobs were on short time. Ford, for example, cut its work force from over 128,000 in March 1929 to approximately 37,000 by August 1939, with the three-day week common. In consequence, Detroit suffered the worst relief crisis of any major city in the country and had the highest unemployment rate. The problem for the city was compounded because, while the Ford plants were not in the city, many of the company's employees lived there. They were thus added to the Detroit relief rolls, rather than to those of Highland Park or Dearborn, when they were laid off. Yet when Detroit officials approached Henry Ford for contributions to their overburdened welfare budget, he refused.

The first labor organization to take an interest in the auto workers' plight was not the AFL but, rather, the IWW. The "Wobblies" had attempted to organize in Detroit much earlier, but their campaign, waged in 1913, had ended in disaster. With the onset of the Depression, they tried again. In the end their efforts were no more effective than they had been twenty years before.

The Communist Party also entered the scene ahead of the AFL. Its members infiltrated the moribund United Auto, Aircraft & Vehicle Workers organization and changed its name to the Auto Workers Union (AWU). The AWU then affiliated with the Trade Union Unity League, a national organization established by the party to rival the AFL. Not many auto workers were attracted to the AWU, but they did join the "hunger marches" it sponsored against the Ford Motor Company in 1932 and 1933. In the first of these, an all-out battle ensued between the marchers and the combined forces of the Dearborn city police and Ford security personnel. Four marchers were killed.

The AWU also assisted in an unsuccessful strike against the Briggs Manufacturing Company in 1933, although the walkout itself was a spontaneous response to a wage cut rather than the result of AWU agitation. In line with a change in Communist Party policy, the AWU went out of existence in 1934. When the Communist Party of America was originally formed, in 1919, it advocated that its members practice "dual unionism"—establish rival organizations to the unions already in existence in the country. In 1921 party members were told to abandon dual unionism and, instead, join the existing unions and achieve leadership positions within them—that is, "bore from within." In 1928 the party again advocated dual unionism, only to reinstate the principle of boring from within in late 1934. It was for that reason that the AWU dissolved itself, and told its members to join one of the other auto unions that were then emerging.

There were a number of strikes by auto workers in the early 1930s. More often than not they were unplanned flare-ups by unorganized workers, although a few did have union direction. The IWW, for example, struck Murray Body in late 1933. Like most such strikes, it failed.

Probably the most important of these walkouts was called by the Mechanics Educational Society of America (MESA), late in 1933, against three GM plants in Flint. Before it ended, the strike had spread to most of the auto plants in Flint, Pontiac, and the Detroit area, with the exception of the Ford Motor Company. It also came to include most of the smaller jobbers in the Detroit area. The MESA organization was composed principally of tool and die makers but once the strike began, MESA made some attempt to broaden membership. The strike was sufficiently effective to delay the introduction of the 1934 models of the struck firms, but its outcome cannot be classified as a real success from the union's point of view. The settlement did result in wage boosts and a measure of union recognition in a few of the smaller Detroit shops but accomplished nothing in the more important plants. Nonetheless, the strike brought out features of the industry that would prove useful to later organizers. The deep-seated hostility to unionism that characterized the industry was highlighted as never before. No matter what form labor organization was to take, the auto industry would not be unionized without a real battle. The MESA strike also underscored the fact that organization would have to be widespread throughout the industry. No matter how scattered the GM plants might be geographically, the corporation was a single employer; however strong the union might be in one plant, if it had no strength elsewhere, it could be undermined. For example, although MESA's strike against GM was relatively effective in Flint, Detroit, and Pontiac, GM could and did shift work to its Toledo and Cleveland plants where MESA had no foothold.

The parts suppliers and small job shops had to be considered too—as they were in the MESA strike—so that work could not be shifted to them, or away from them if they were the only object of pressure.

The strike also made clear GM's position as the giant of the industry. As a GM official himself said early in the strike, whatever the corporation did affected the whole auto complex.

At best, the AFL remained on the sidelines during the labor activity of the early 1930s and, in the case of the MESA strike, was actually hostile. The Federation looked upon MESA as an "outlaw" union that threatened the jurisdictional autonomy of the International Association of Machinists—this despite the IAM's lack of success in organizing tool and die makers in the industry.

The dramatic change in the federal government's attitude toward organized labor finally brought the AFL out of its hole. The shift in attitude was foreshadowed in 1932 when the large number of Democratic congressmen elected in 1930 helped to pass the Norris-LaGuardia Act. By its terms, the federal courts were severely limited in their powers to issue anti-strike injunctions. In addition, so-called yellow dog contracts, which had become very fashionable among employers, by which a job applicant had to pledge not to join a union as a condition of employment, could no longer be enforced in the federal courts.

More important was the passage of the National Industrial Recovery Act (NIRA) in 1933. That legislation, designed to help both businessmen and wage earners, permitted industries to establish their own codes of fair competition and was intended to eliminate indiscriminate price and wage cutting. At the same time, section 7 (a) of the NIRA guaranteed to workers the right to bargain collectively through representatives of their own choosing, free from employer interference. This constituted a landmark for organized labor, and, with its passage, the AFL decided to try once more to organize the auto industry. The plan provided that auto workers be placed in local bodies directly affiliated with the Federation. As it worked out, there was usually one such local in each plant.

The drive had hard going. The jurisdictional concerns voiced by the older craft unions continued as a problem. The auto workers themselves were fearful that in the end the AFL would, indeed, parcel them out among the various craft unions. As one man put it, this would pit one powerful battleship (the employer) against "lots of little rowboats" that could be picked off one at a time. The campaign also suffered from a lack of funds and from the Federation's cautious approach to the use of the strike. Given the employers' hostile attitude toward unionization, the AFL should have been more militant than it was. With the specter of unemployment everpresent, workers were wary of joining a labor organization since it could so easily lead to discharge. Since, in addition, they mistrusted the AFL, it is not surprising that they did not rush to join its ranks.

A number of the manufacturers quickly established company unions after the NIRA was enacted as a means of offering lip service to section 7 (a). Then, when the AFL asked for a hearing on its members' complaints, management could respond that there already was a union in existence that adequately represented the workers, and that the AFL should process grievances through it. Later, industry representatives changed their tone and agreed to meet with AFL representatives and any other accredited group or any individual employee who preferred to bargain for himself. The AFL insisted that the organization that represented a majority of the workers in a given unit should be given sole collective bargaining rights, but this the employers refused to concede.

By the spring of 1934 the question of representation and disputes on other issues (particularly discrimination against union members) had become quite heated. When the AFL threatened a widespread strike, President Franklin D. Roosevelt stepped into the situation. This, in fact, had been the purpose of the strike threat because the leaders of the AFL organizational drive were fairly certain that their union was still too weak to stage a successful walkout. They banked on the fact that the auto industry was so vital to the recovery of the nation's economy that the government would step in at the mere suggestion of a strike rather than allow a work stoppage.

As a result of Roosevelt's efforts, a compromise was reached in March 1934. One result was the establishment of a presidentially appointed tripartite Automobile Labor Board (ALB), empowered to intervene in cases of alleged discrimination due to union membership. The ALB was also charged with ensuring employee representation by means of bargaining committees. All employees, whether members of outside unions, company organizations, or unaffiliated, were represented on these committees in accordance with the relative strength of their group among all workers in the bargaining unit. The fact that the auto industry operated under a system of proportional representation made it unique among the hundreds of industries covered by NIRA codes. The rest accorded exclusive bargaining rights to the majority organization.

The ALB was abolished in 1935 when the Supreme Court found the NIRA unconstitutional. Even before that, the board had been effectively discredited in the eyes of the auto workers, who found it too slow-moving and not sufficiently protective of employee interests in cases of alleged discrimination. Nonetheless, the bargaining committees, set up under the board's sponsorship, did at least provide some experience in collective bargaining to men wholly innocent of the process until then and produced a nucleus of potential leadership for the future.

The demise of the NIRA did not signal a change in governmental policy toward the organization of labor. The National Labor Relations Act (the Wagner Act), enacted in 1935, incorporated section 7 (a) of the old NIRA. The ALB experience, particularly, convinced the drafters of the new legislation that plural representation caused too much confusion and strife. Thus they endorsed the principle of exclusive representation and incorporated it into the Wagner Act.

Despite the shortcomings of the Automobile Labor Board, worker interest in independent unionization was stimulated during its short lifetime. Initially, unions independent of the AFL benefitted most from that interest. MESA was one of them. The Hudson-based Associated Automobile Workers of America (AAWA), a secessionist group from the AFL, was another. A third, the Automotive Industrial Workers Association (AIWA), was the outgrowth of mixed bargaining agencies set up during the ALB period in the Detroit-area Chrysler plants. By 1935 the AIWA had spread to other plants around the Motor City as well. In August of that year, when the AFL finally agreed to form its directly affiliated auto locals into a separately chartered organization, the new union it formed—the United Automobile Workers of America (UAW)—had under 26,000 members. That figure represented about 6 percent of all organizable workers in the industry. However, the UAW had only about 2000 members in Michigan, the heart of the industry. In contrast, the independents together had at least as many members as the UAW, and their strength lay in Michigan, particularly in Detroit.

During the first year of its existence, the UAW was still under the protective wing of the AFL. Despite vehement protests from UAW members, the Federation appointed the new union's chief officers, who continued to follow the AFL's cautious policies. Hostility to AFL domination became so marked during the year that the Federation's executive council finally agreed to permit UAW members to elect their own leaders at the 1936 annual convention. A month after that convention, the entire membership of the Chrysler-based AIWA, much of the Hudson

independent (the AAWA), and some MESA affiliates joined
UAW ranks. In July 1936 the UAW in turn affiliated with a
new aggressive wing of the AFL, the Committee for Industrial
Organization (CIO). In joining the CIO the UAW clearly
indicated its commitment to industrial unionism, because the
CIO itself had been formed to combat the view of the majority
of the AFL leaders that craft union jurisdiction must be safe-
guarded at all costs. The CIO group, in contrast, believed that
workers in mass production industries had to be organized on
an industrywide basis. The argument over policy had come to a
head at the 1935 AFL convention. Symbolic of the rift was a
sharp exchange between John L. Lewis, head of the United
Mine Workers and chief spokesman for the newer view, and
William L. ("Big Bill") Hutcheson,* head of the Carpenters.
Their argument ended when Lewis socked Hutcheson in the
jaw.

By the time the UAW joined the CIO, feeling between CIO
members and the AFL old guard was so strong that the Federation was demanding that the CIO disband. A few months
later, the AFL would suspend the mavericks, and the CIO,
renamed the Congress of Industrial Organization, would go its
own way. The AFL and CIO would not reunite again for
almost twenty years.

Once the UAW affiliated with the CIO, it immediately began
to receive help and advice from Lewis and other seasoned,
militant leaders of the parent organization and stepped up its
organizing efforts at once. Moreover, the automobile industry
was beginning to recover from the effects of the Depression, and
employment was up. This served as an additional impetus to
the new union, for it made collective pressure on companies
more effective.

---

* In a book on Michigan labor history, it is appropriate to point out that
Hutcheson was a Michigan product, born in the Saginaw Valley in 1874 during the lumber boom days described in Chapter 2. He served his apprentice-
ship as a carpenter in Bay City. He developed an early interest in labor
organization, traveling to Detroit as a boy to hear Richard Trevellick and,
as a teenager, was an eager member of the audience when Gompers spoke
in Saginaw in 1888. His first experience as a union organizer came in Midland, Michigan (1904), and after he was blacklisted there he moved on to
organize in Saginaw. By 1915 he was president of the United Brotherhood of
Carpenters and Joiners.

Worker grievances were numerous, and the militant little union was quick to play on them. Employment in the industry was irregular, peaking in the late fall and early winter, as new models came off the line, and slacking off by early summer. Thus while the worker earned a high daily wage, his annual earnings could be as low as $600 or less. Layoff and rehire were not necessarily governed by seniority; instead they often depended upon the foreman's whim. Companies lowered piece rates when the work force boosted its output, and the "speed-up" of the assembly line was also not uncommon. All of these factors led to tensions and uneasiness that made most autoworkers willing to give the UAW organizers a favorable hearing.

The new union was definitely not reluctant to use the strike, and, indeed, a large measure of its success derived from the able use of a variant on that technique, the sit-down strike.*

The sit-down strike had a number of advantages over the traditional walk-out, especially for a union as new and small as the UAW. An aggressive minority could gain control of and hold a plant far more easily than if it had attempted to control entry into the plant from the outside. Once inside, defense from strikebreakers or police was less difficult since points of entry were limited and the strikers less vulnerable to attack than they would have been on the picket line. In the event that an employer attempted to oust the strikers by force, his own property was likely to be damaged. He could also be charged with at least part of the blame for any violence and damage that might ensue and run the risk of public disapproval. The sit-down was, in addition, an excellent organizing technique. Once a union had control of the exits, the employees still inside were a "captive audience," in a sense. Some who had not joined the

---

* The UAW was not the first to use the sit-down technique. Claim has been made that that device was used as far back as 3700 B.C. in Egypt; and there is definite evidence that it was used in France in the late Middle Ages. The first "stay-in" in the United States is supposed to have been staged by some Cincinnati brewery workers in 1884, and the IWW used the technique against General Electric in Schenectady, N. Y., in 1906. The device then fell into disuse in this country until November, 1933, when it was used against the Hormel Packing Company in Austin, Minnesota. Following that, the sit-down strike came back into favor and was used extensively by labor unions throughout the country.

union before succumbed to the enthusiasm of the moment. Others, initially less convinced, responded to group pressure. One way or the other, a union's membership expanded rapidly. Of utmost importance, by halting production altogether the union could exert maximum pressure on the employer to submit to its demands.

In November 1936 the UAW called its first extensive sit-down strike, against the Bendix Corporation in South Bend, Indiana. After nine days, the union won recognition as bargaining agent for its members, a grievance procedure, two hours call-in pay, and a day's notice on layoff. The next month sit-downs wrested concessions from the Midland Steel Frame Company and the Kelsey-Hayes Wheel Company in Detroit. Interestingly enough, the Ford Motor Company played a major role in the Detroit strikes on behalf of the UAW. The two companies were Ford suppliers, and the auto manufacturer pressured them into settling rather than see its own production suffer.

The experience gained in such strikes proved valuable to the UAW, but union strategists knew that if the UAW were to make an impact in the automobile industry, it had to do battle with General Motors, Chrysler, and Ford. By 1936 the three companies together controlled 89 percent of the passenger car market. Organizing only the other 11 percent would hardly make a dent in the industry and, additionally, might well hurt the smaller companies' competitive position.

In determining overall strategy against the Big Three, it was clear that the first move could not be against the Ford Motor Company. That firm had been virtually the only one in the industry which had not signed the now defunct automobile code; and while it had complied with most of the code's terms, Ford had pointedly refused to make any effective gestures in the direction of section 7 (a). Thus the company established neither company unions nor the mixed bargaining agencies of the ALB period. Added to the Ford workers' lack of collective bargaining experience was the company's pronounced hostility to unionization and an effective espionage system. As a result, the UAW had made virtually no headway in the Ford plants.

Although the union's greatest strength lay in the Chrysler Corporation plants, thanks to the numbers brought into the

UAW by the AIWA, the leaders decided not to approach that firm first. Gaining concessions from Chrysler did not necessarily mean that GM would follow suit and, in fact, might have increased GM's hostility to unionism. If, on the other hand, concessions could be obtained from GM, Chrysler, with its reputation for greater tolerance toward labor organizations, might be persuaded to bargain with the UAW without the need of a strike. This was a major consideration for a new union with a small treasury.

In devising their strategy, the UAW leaders had the benefit not only of the lessons learned in the MESA strike, but also those learned in connection with a strike against the Toledo Chevrolet plants in 1935. The Toledo plants produced all Chevrolet and Pontiac transmissions at that time. The strike brought Chevrolet production to a complete halt, but Pontiac production continued since the work on transmissions for that model was transferred to the Buick plant in Flint. (This, incidentally, was one reason the auto workers came to want their own union: it was the AFL leaders who had persuaded the members of the Buick local to continue production rather than join the strike.) As a result of the Toledo strike, the union won a measure of recognition from GM—but the corporation, too, had learned a lesson during the course of the strike. It subsequently transferred about 50 percent of the machinery from the Toledo plant to Saginaw and Muncie.

Organizational activity began in earnest in the GM plants in June 1936. The plan worked out by the UAW leaders and their CIO advisers called for a concentration of organizational activity in key plants within the corporation's system—units which, if shut down, could effectively close the rest of GM's plants. The leaders at national headquarters had not yet reached their organizing goal, however, when in late December 1936 the GM strike began.

In many respects the strike could not have come at a worse time. The CIO was in the midst of its campaign to organize the steel industry. With the outbreak of the GM strike, it faced the necessity of waging war on two fronts. In addition, the strategists had not planned to move against GM at least until after January 1, 1937, when Democrat Frank Murphy would be inaugurated as governor of Michigan, in the hope that a Democratic administration would be more sympathetic to them. But the restlessness of the auto workers and their local leaders forced their hand. Impatience among the GM workers was already evident in November and mid-December when sit-down strikes broke out in plants in Atlanta and Kansas City. That impatience heightened in late December when top GM officials refused to meet with UAW president Homer Martin. They told him flatly to take up any complaints at the local level. Thus it took only a rather minor incident to touch things off.

On December 28, 1936, at the Fisher Body plant in Cleveland, where all Chevrolet stampings were produced, management representatives postponed a meeting with local union leaders, scheduled for that morning, until the afternoon. In response, the union called a sit-down strike. Two days later, on December 30, alleged discrimination against some employees because of union membership caused workers in Fisher Body No. 2 in Flint to follow suit. Later the same day, when fellow employees at Fisher Body No. 1 heard rumors that the company was moving dies out of the buildings, they joined in as well.* Fisher No. 1 produced all stampings for Cadillacs, Buicks, Oldsmobiles, and Pontiacs and was thus a key plant in the GM network. When the workers in that plant sat down, the UAW's strike against the General Motors Corporation was on in earnest. Within a week 13 other plants in the GM complex struck as well. As a result within two weeks almost all of the corporation's 69 plants had to close, and 112,800 production workers (of a total of some 150,000) were idle. By early February 1937 production, which had reached 53,000 units a week in mid-December 1936, had tumbled to 1,500.

Though UAW and CIO leaders did not like the timing of the strike, they decided to get behind the strikers and soon formulated demands to submit to GM officials. Chief among these was

* Recent evidence that has come to light indicates that the rumor concerning the die-moving may well have been false and deliberately planted by the local leaders in order to foment the strike. The flat-glass workers were then striking, and the Flint leaders feared that a window glass shortage would force the closing of the plants in any event in a few days. Therefore, they may have spread the rumor in order to take the initiative in closing down the plant.

that GM recognize the UAW, at the national level, as the exclusive bargaining agent for all GM employees. In seeking exclusive recognition, the union did not press the claim that such recognition was a right, under the terms of the Wagner Act, due it as majority representative. In fact, the UAW had signed up only a small number of GM employees. Even if the union had represented a majority, it could not have relied upon protection under the act since the constitutionality of that legislation was still very much in doubt. Moreover, GM had already given notice in another connection that even if the Wagner Act were upheld in the courts, the corporation should not be construed as an industry in interstate commerce within the meaning of the act.

When the sit-down strike began, GM representatives emphasized that they would not bargain with the UAW at all until

The General Motors sit-down strike at Flint, 1937

the plants were evacuated, and then only at the individual plant level. As to the union's demand for sole collective bargaining rights, that was tantamount to a request for a closed shop, they said, and was thus out of the question.

At GM's request, the Genesee County circuit court issued an injunction on January 2, 1937, requiring that the Flint strikers evacuate the plants. Public support of the injunction was undermined, however, when, three days later, the union announced that the judge who had issued the injunction owned 3,665 shares of GM stock with a market value of $219,900. After that revelation, the corporation decided not to press the matter for the time being.

Frank Murphy, by then governor of Michigan, made attempts almost from the beginning of the strike to bring the parties together but ran into stiff opposition from GM. Even when the UAW agreed to drop its exclusive representation demand as a precondition to negotiations and to settle for talks at the national level, GM refused to discuss the matter until the plants were emptied. Nor would the corporation promise that it would not resume operations once the men were out. Governor Murphy chided GM and pointed out that the blame for the sit-downs rested upon the employers' shoulders. He later wrote that by refusing to negotiate they forced the workers to use "the only effective weapon they could find, the Sit-Down strike." It should be noted that at the time the courts had not yet ruled on the legality or illegality of the sit-down.

GM would have none of that argument. On January 11 it ordered that the heat be turned off and food be kept from the strikers at the Fisher No. 2 plant in Flint—the one plant in which strikers did not have possession of the entire plant and did not control the gates. The besieged strikers fought back and captured the gates from the company guards. The Flint police were then called in. The men in the plant, with the help of outside sympathizers, successfully fought them off as well by showering them with car door hinges and anything else they could lay their hands on. In the end the police retreated. Victory in this "Battle of the Running Bulls," as it came to be known, had a marked effect upon the entire labor movement in Michigan. The UAW's fight against GM now became all labor's battle against the automotive giant. The Detroit *Labor News* exulted in banner headlines that "G.M. NO LONGER OWNS THE GOVT OF MICHIGAN" and thanked the Flint strikers for giving renewed courage to labor everywhere.

Immediately after the "battle," Governor Murphy ordered the National Guard to Flint. He called out the Guard not to evict the strikers but, rather, to maintain the status quo and ensure that no further violence ensued. To General Motors, its property rights might be inalienable and the strikers lawless trespassers, but as the governor viewed the situation, there was much more at stake. As he later explained, "Civil war was imminent. ... The dynamite was ready, only a spark was needed to supply an explosion that would have terrorized the entire nation." It was up to him to see to it that that spark did not fly. The union and the company had to be brought together to work things out peaceably. In the interim, the guardsmen were to maintain law and order.

After much effort the governor persuaded GM to meet with the UAW and, on January 15, 1937, an agreement was finally reached. The union was to evacuate the plants on January 17, and GM was not to resume operations for a two-week period during which negotiations were to take place.

Strikers left some of the plants before the union learned that W. S. Knudsen, executive vice-president of General Motors, had also agreed to bargain with the "Flint Alliance," a back-to-work organization apparently formed with GM's blessing to counteract the UAW. Upon hearing this, the Flint sit-downers, who had been preparing to leave, refused to budge. This brought negotiations to a standstill. Alfred P. Sloan, Jr., president of the corporation, did agree, however, to meet with Secretary of Labor Frances Perkins in Washington. Secretary Perkins hoped to bring Sloan together with John L. Lewis, but her efforts were futile. Sloan refused to discuss the matter with Lewis until the plants were cleared. This brought forth Lewis' famous statement that "for six months [during the presidential election campaign,] the economic royalists represented by General Motors contributed their money and used their energy to drive this administration from power. The administration asked labor for help to repel this attack, and labor gave its help. The same economic royalists now have their fangs in labor. The workers of this country expect the administration to help the workers in every legal way, and to support the auto workers in the General Motors plants."

General Motors took the offensive against the UAW again and succeeded in reopening some of its plants. At this the union leaders decided upon a desperate piece of strategy to regain the upper hand. They let it be known that on February 1 they planned to occupy the Chevrolet No. 9 plant in Flint. At the appointed time company police scurried to that plant to ward off the attack while, nearby, the union engaged in taking its real objective, the Chevrolet No. 4 plant. Chevy No. 4 produced all Chevrolet engines and was therefore a key unit in the GM complex.

The day after the union captured Chevy No. 4, GM again requested and received a court order to evict the strikers—this time from a judge who was not a GM stockholder. Evacuation was ordered for February 3, 1937, but that day passed, and the strikers remained in the plants. Two days later, the judge issued a writ of attachment ordering the sheriff to "attach the bodies" of those involved in the strike. The sheriff contacted Governor Murphy, who, hoping to get the parties together and stalling for time, asked the sheriff to wait. At this point, President Roosevelt finally persuaded Knudsen to meet with Lewis. At the same time, Governor Murphy made it clear to Lewis that if these meetings failed, he would demand that the plants be evacuated.

The parties finally reached an agreement on February 11, 1937. By its terms, GM agreed to sign a national contract with the UAW, the first such agreement the corporation had ever signed. The company further agreed to recognize the union as the bargaining agent for its members in the 82 plants in the GM system which had not directly participated in the strike. In the 17 plants which had struck, the union received a good deal more, what amounted to sole collective bargaining rights for a period of six months. GM agreed, in addition, to reemploy the strikers and not to discriminate against UAW members. While the union could not actively solicit members on corporation premises, GM did agree to permit UAW members to hold "individual discussions" with employees inside the plants. In return, the UAW agreed to evacuate the plants and promised not to strike during the life of the agreement.

The UAW had won a major victory: a national agreement with the largest of the Big Three and sole recognition in some of its plants. At the same time, it had undergone an internal leadership crisis during the negotiations, which was to plague it for some time. Homer Martin, UAW president, had proved to be an erratic and inept negotiator, and the week before the settlement was reached, his cohorts had been forced to hustle him out of town. As a result the only UAW official to sign the February 11 agreement was Wyndham Mortimer, first vice-president of the union. Since Mortimer had been a key man in organizing the Flint workers, this constituted a personal victory for him. At the same time, it was deflating to Martin's ego and, more important,· a blow to his reputation as a competent leader.

On the surface, however, everything had gone smoothly. David had taken Goliath and was pleased.

"Goliath" capitulated for a number of reasons. The longer the strike lasted, the more it hurt the corporation financially. GM sales in February 1937 were the lowest for that month since 1933, and the company had been forced to reduce its dividends. Reportedly, the strike cost the corporation a million dollars a day in potential sales.

In addition, public hostility to GM, which was already evident, grew stronger still when the U.S. Senate's La Follette Civil Liberties Committee revealed that the company had been spending thousands of dollars every year on labor espionage. Car sales depended too much on a good "public image" for GM to continue to use strong-arm methods against the union on its own and it had come to the conclusion that it was not going to get the governor to take that sort of action on its behalf. This put the company in a very awkward position. Nor was it Governor Murphy alone who was uncooperative. GM could not count on the other automobile manufacturers either. It was alleged that when GM requested the other automobile companies to lock out their employees, in order to create a united front against the UAW, they had not only refused, but stepped up production. The Chrysler Corporation went so far as to announce a 10 percent wage increase on February 9 to forestall labor difficulties in its own plants. If GM had hoped that strikes in the flat-glass industry would cause a shortage of car windows, thus forcing its competitors to close, and perhaps encouraging them to cooperate, it was doomed to disappointment because those strikes were settled. It really had no choice; it had to come to terms.

Governor Murphy's part in bringing the parties together and persuading them to compromise their positions should not be underestimated, and it was not at the time. Corporation and UAW officials praised him; the public acclaimed him. He was the hero of the hour who, almost singlehandedly, had averted disaster.

The UAW now turned its attention to the Chrysler Corpora-

Michigan governor Frank Murphy, left, and John L. Lewis during the 1937 auto negotiations

tion. In contrast to GM's refusal to grant a national level conference, the Chrysler people immediately agreed to hold one. While the union pressed a number of demands at that meeting, the key issue was sole bargaining rights in the entire Chrysler system. This the company would not concede.

Consequently, on March 8, 1937, the Chrysler sit-down strike began. Within a matter of days all Chrysler plants, nationwide, ceased production, and its 68,525 employees were idle. A number of Chrysler suppliers, with some additional 29,600 workers, were affected as well.

Because of the number of strikers involved in the sit-down, the Chrysler strike has been called the largest sit-down strike in American history. However, not all those initially involved in the sit-down remained inside the plants for the duration of the strike. The food supply problem alone would have made that impracticable and, in addition, there were duties, such as manning picket lines, that needed to be performed on the outside.

The UAW had assumed that Chrysler would capitulate quickly rather than run the risk of losing some of its market to its competitors. But the company held firm. Beyond this, the public sympathized less with the union's efforts against Chrysler than it had during the GM strike. In part, this was due to Chrysler's policies toward the strikers. It carefully avoided the mistakes made in Flint. It supplied heat, water, and electricity to the struck plants, at company expense, throughout the strike. It never called in the police. Moreover, at one point some high UAW officials made the statement that the union had enough members at Chrysler to entitle it to "closed shop conditions." While in fact the UAW was not demanding the closed shop, Chrysler could and did capitalize on that and similar statements to try to show that this was the real purpose behind the sit-down.

Another factor added to public disenchantment. The Chrysler sit-down was not the only one plaguing the state at the time. In Detroit alone there were so many that the city's newspapers ran daily "box scores" on them. A Detroit newspaperman commented that, "Sitting down has replaced baseball as a national pastime, and sitter-downers clutter up the landscape in every direction." The day the Chrysler strike began, for example, Hudson Motor workers sat down too. A few days later sit-downs occurred in aluminum, iron smelting, and packing plants; in department, drug, grocery, and clothing stores; in cigar factories and a welfare office. Hotel employees joined in, and famous show business people had the option of walking down twelve or more flights of stairs, luggage and all, or hopefully waiting it out.

The state of Michigan was getting a black eye all over the country. Firms threatened to leave; others allegedly changed their plans to come. In an editorial entitled "Oh, Michigan!" *The New York Times* complained: "Isn't that uneasy peninsula between the lakes the place where all the trouble that afflicts this nation starts? Didn't the banking panic of 1933 rear its ugly head in Michigan and slither madly across the rest of the country? And haven't we now a plague of sit-down strikes made and patented in Michigan and ready to export?" The editorial went on to suggest that Governor Murphy resign and hand over the state to John L. Lewis "as a kind of mandated territory." Michigan could then isolate itself "as a social laboratory devoted exclusively to Mr. Lewis's experiments." The harried governor, the hero of the General Motors strike, now became a chief target of criticism.

Governor Murphy moved quickly to get negotiations going between Walter Chrysler and John L. Lewis and made it clear to Lewis that this time he would be much less reluctant to use force to clear the plants of sit-downers. On March 24 Lewis agreed to the evacuation of the plants with the understanding that the Chrysler Corporation would not attempt to resume production until an agreement had been reached. The following day the men left the plants, and the biggest sit-down of them all was over.

The settlement itself, reached April 6, was a compromise. The Chrysler Corporation agreed to recognize the UAW at the national level as the bargaining agent—but only for UAW members, not for all Chrysler employees. The union demand for sole recognition had thus officially been denied. The company did, however, promise that it would not "aid, promote or finance" any other labor organization, nor make an agreement with one "for the purpose of undermining" the UAW. Privately, Chrysler representatives also assured Lewis that they would never require the union to show how many members it actually had and that it would operate as if the UAW represented all Chrysler employees.

While this was clearly a step forward for the UAW, it was a disappointment to the more militant members of the union, and the strike leaders had a hard time "selling" the agreement to the members. The mixed reaction to the Chrysler settlement added fuel to the factional fights that continued to plague the UAW through much of its early history. Yet with the signing of the Chrysler agreement, the second of the Big Three had fallen. Within days, a sit-down strike at the Reo Truck plant in Lansing and the Hudson Motor strike were settled on much the same terms as the Chrysler agreement. One by one the auto companies "fell." By July 1937 the UAW could claim 370,000 members and some 400 signed contracts Only the Ford fortress eluded it, not to be stormed until 1941. By mid-1937 the union's power base had also shifted, so that its main strength was in Michigan, the heart of the industry. Detroit alone had 200,000 UAW members.

The Chrysler strike not only accelerated unionization in the auto industry but did much to organize all of Detroit. Unionization came not just because the rest of Detroit followed Chrysler's example. UAW leaders and CIO organizers actively aided other Detroit workers in their unionizing efforts. They offered their services on the picket line and acted as advisors during negotiations. Often, however, there was no need to volunteer such help. A spontaneous sit-down would be followed by a phone call to UAW headquarters asking for help. One morning when August ("Gus") Scholle, then a CIO organizer, arrived at his office, he found a whole plant's work force camping on his doorstep clamoring for a CIO charter.

With the end of the Chrysler strike, the era of the sit-down virtually came to a close. The biggest had, for all practical purposes, been the last. In part this was due to the labor movement's recognition that the public had become less tolerant of the technique. Probably a more powerful reason was that the U. S. Supreme Court upheld the Wagner Act, and unions now had easier and more acceptable means of gaining recognition.

In 1939 the U. S. Supreme Court handed down its decision on the legality of sit-down strikes in *NLRB* vs. *Fansteel Metallurgical Corporation*. The Court dealt sternly with this abuse of property rights. Sit-down strikes were illegal, and workers and unions using this technique forfeited all right to the protection of the law. The leaders of the UAW could not have been unduly alarmed. It no longer mattered. Industrial unionism had already come to the automobile industry.

After its initial victories the UAW underwent a period of internal strife that nearly tore it apart. In part the in-fighting was due to the fact that a number of aggressive, able young men who had risen quickly in the new organization, had gathered a fiercely loyal following around them, and were jock-

Supporters hoist Walter Reuther to their shoulders after his first election to the presidency of the UAW in 1946. On the left in the striped tie is his brother, Roy.

eying for position. But the fight involved more than personalities. Among its members the UAW contained highly vocal minorities representing right-wing and left-wing Communists, as well as several varieties of Socialists; and the factional fights within the union also reflected these differences in political ideology.* These ideological wrangles affected not only the UAW but a number of other CIO unions as well and were finally resolved only after World War II.

It was not until the late 1940s that the late Walter Reuther emerged as a leader strong enough to win the loyalty of a sufficiently large number of UAW members to overcome the ideological fratricide within the union. Thereafter, the "United" Auto Workers was no longer a misnomer.

Today, the small "David" that dared to defy Goliath is the second largest union in the nation, a giant organization of about 1.5 million members, who are spread throughout the auto, agricultural implement, and aerospace industries. The goals it has sought for its members, the imaginative bargaining techniques it has developed to achieve them, and its wider social concerns have consistently attracted national attention and have made the UAW one of the leading spokesmen for the labor movement, and workers generally, on the current American scene.

* This aspect of the factional fight within the UAW is ably covered in Walter Galenson's book, *The CIO Challenge to the AFL* (Cambridge, 1960), pp. 150-57.

6

MICHIGAN LABOR IN POLITICS

On July 6, 1854, some 1200 men gathered in Jackson, Michigan, to found a new political party. They first crowded into a room in the city hall but soon moved outside to the less stifling atmosphere of a nearby oak grove. There they drew up a platform for the new organization and decided on the party's first slate of candidates for statewide public office—the list of nominees for Michigan's off-year elections. That fledgling organization, formally launched in a clump of Michigan trees, was the Republican Party.

The slate drawn up in Jackson was victorious in the fall elections, and Michigan rarely deserted the GOP thereafter for nearly a hundred years. From the 1854 election until the Great Depression, the winner of the Republican nomination for any statewide or congressional office in Michigan was almost certain to be elected. Democrats were able to place their man in the governorship only four times during the period: and only once—in 1890—did they gain control of the state legislature. In short, until the 1930s—and even beyond—Michigan for all practical purposes could be considered a one-party state. The modern history of Michigan politics is one of the gradual depletion of this immense reservoir of Republican votes.

Public reaction to the effects of the Depression, as expressed at the polls, hurt the Republican Party in Michigan as it did throughout much of the nation. Nonetheless, the GOP remained a formidable force in the state throughout the 1930s and 1940s. The Republicans still retained control of the state legislature and continued to send their candidates to Congress by a better than two-to-one margin over their opponents. Between 1932 and 1946 they won the governorship five times to the Democrats' three.

The real turning point in Democratic Party fortunes came in 1948 when organized labor in Michigan forged a formal alliance with a group of liberal Democrats and moved into the political arena more forcibly than ever before. From that time to this Michigan has been a two-party state, a real political battleground with victory for either party's candidates a matter of genuine contention.

HISTORICAL BACKGROUND

Michigan labor was no newcomer to politics in 1948. Like organized labor generally in the United States, its representatives were always politically aware. City and state central bodies had busily engaged in guarding labor's interests as soon as they were formed. The Knights of Labor developed a broad political program. And even the avowedly apolitical Michigan Federation of Labor was actively lobbying and electioneering. But by comparison those early efforts were meager compared to labor's political role in recent times. Moreover, they were usually ineffectual. When an effective piece of labor legislation was enacted, it was often due as much to middle-class pressure upon lawmakers as to labor's lobbying efforts. For example, Michigan's first workmen's compensation legislation, enacted in 1912, was preceded by almost a decade of mounting public insistence that employers adequately compensate their employees for job-related injuries and fatalities. When the law was passed, the Michigan Manufacturers' Association had already been won over to that point of view and was at least as responsible for pushing the bill through the legislature as was the Michigan Federation of Labor.

Overall, particularly during the period of AFL dominance, labor's political efforts were essentially negative: the main objective was to ensure minimum governmental interference in trade union activity rather than to promote active governmental participation on labor's behalf. In addition, the legislation sponsored or endorsed by organized labor covered a narrow range of topics. It focused largely on health and safety measures or was designed to protect women and children in the work force. The adult male was to look to his union, not the state, for help. One dramatic illustration of this attitude was that the nation was well into the Great Depression before the AFL would endorse unemployment insurance legislation—and then only after a stiff battle at its 1932 convention.

The picture began to change once the CIO was established. The heads of the new industrial unions recognized that in large measure their organizations owed their existence to the New Deal. Thus as early as 1936 they were ready not only to endorse Roosevelt's renomination but to contribute heavily in time and money to his campaign.

In the spring of 1936 John L. Lewis and other labor leaders created a political arm, Labor's Non-Partisan League (LNPL). The LNPL sponsored radio broadcasts, distributed campaign literature, and held rallies. It is estimated that, all told, trade unions contributed almost $750,000 to the Democratic Party during the course of the campaign.

The old guard AFL chieftains were reluctant to make so firm a commitment to Roosevelt, although some Federation affiliates did cooperate with the LNPL and contributed to its coffers. In part, AFL hesitation was simply a reflection of its hostility to the CIO. Beyond that, however, in a traditionally Republican area such as Michigan, Federation representatives had, over time, developed a working relationship with GOP state and local officials, particularly with regard to patronage matters, and were thus wary of moving into the opposition camp.

Even within the ranks of the industrial unions, the CIO's all-out endorsement of the New Deal met with a certain amount of opposition. Some of the new unions believed that they were now powerful enough to take independent political action. Sentiment in this direction was so strong among UAW members, for example, that CIO officials had to pressure the delegates to the 1936 autoworkers convention before they could be persuaded to endorse Roosevelt.

In 1940 John L. Lewis resigned as president of the CIO and took Labor's Non-Partisan League with him back to the United Mine Workers. The gap thus created was filled in 1943 when the CIO created its own political arm, the Political Action Committee, or CIO-PAC. The CIO-PAC began to function at once in connection with the 1944 presidential campaign. Under the direction of Sidney Hillman, president of the Amalgamated Clothing Workers of America, the new organization developed a network of regional centers. Those, in turn, worked through the affiliated union locals at the grass roots level. When Roosevelt was reelected, the "Hillman Blitz" was widely credited with his margin of victory.

Michigan went to the Republican Thomas Dewey in 1944, however. The CIO-PAC had made some inroads in the industrial area in and around Detroit but was ineffective in much of the rest of the state.* Even in Detroit it suffered a setback the following year when the CIO-PAC candidate for mayor, UAW Vice-President Richard Frankensteen, was defeated. Nonetheless, the opposition press gave grudging credit to CIO-PAC's efforts to register Detroit voters and get them to the polls on election day. The then-conservative *New York Times* concluded that if the CIO had been allied with a political party in that election, it would have been unbeatable. For the time being, however, the CIO in Michigan preferred to remain "nonpartisan."

The 1945 race was not the first in which labor had run a candidate for mayor of Detroit. In 1937 the CIO put up its own man for mayor and ran five UAW notables (including Walter Reuther) for the Common Council. The slate did well in the primaries, but lost in November after a concerted effort on the

---

* Sections of the Upper Peninsula also voted Democratic. That area, in fact, was the first in the state to drift to the Democratic column. As far back as 1928, Delta County had been the only Michigan county to register a majority of votes for Al Smith for President.

part of the city newspapers to equate its election with a John L. Lewis "takeover" that would turn Detroit into an experimental laboratory to test out Communist doctrine.

As early as 1939, when the Michigan CIO held its first convention, the majority of the delegates had fought off attempts at independent third-party political action on the ground that the New Dealers deserved support. As one man put it: "we are not going to sacrifice the people who have created the labor relations bill [the Wagner Act], unemployment insurance, social security, wages and hours, and we are not going to go against these forces to build a third party until we see there is no hope along that line." At the same time, it was made clear that endorsement of the New Dealers who had been sympathetic to labor's interests was not to be construed as an all-out endorsement of the Democratic Party as a whole. Rather, it was an effort to support the "progressive" forces within the party. Indeed, at that first convention the resolution concerning the 1940 presidential campaign made no mention of a political party whatever. Instead, it simply indicated support for whichever presidential candidate continued to carry out the policies initiated by President Roosevelt and his administration. This brand of "nonpartisanship" remained policy until 1948.

Labor's political efforts really came of age after Congress passed the Labor-Management Relations (Taft-Hartley) Act of 1947 over President Truman's veto. Its enactment really drove home to union leadership the fact that organized labor's stake in politics was substantial and permanent, involving the possible loss of all the gains labor had made since the Great Depression. For example, Section 14 (b) of the act, which enabled states to forbid union shop agreements, was widely viewed by labor as nothing less than a declaration of war against organized labor itself. This became particularly clear when in many states the advocates of the "right-to-work" laws often joined forces with those opposed to the minimum wage, improvements in unemployment compensation, and, in some areas, the introduction and enactment of civil rights legislation.

The Taft-Hartley Act was directly responsible for the creation of Labor's League for Political Education (LLPE), the AFL counterpart to the CIO-PAC. This constituted a marked departure from the AFL's earlier attitude toward political action and acknowledged that the Federation, too, had to be active in the political arena. Representatives of labor's two political arms usually worked closely together after the LLPE was formed until their parent organizations merged in 1955. The two were then combined into a new political organization, the AFL-CIO's Committee on Political Education, or COPE.

It was in the setting of the Taft-Hartley setback that the Michigan labor movement abandoned nonpartisanship. It was reported that early in 1948 Gus Scholle, then simultaneously president of the Michigan CIO, chairman of the state CIO-PAC and CIO Regional Director, had declared, "I now think that in the interests of simplifying the mechanics of voting, that the CIO should endorse only Democrats, [and] endorse no one for any office where a Democratic candidate is unacceptable." While the story may be apocryphal (Scholle later denied

Gus Scholle during the early CIO organizing days.

it), it nevertheless sums up the shift that actually took place. Shortly thereafter, at its annual convention, the Michigan CIO announced its open support of the Democratic Party.

Even then, it was stressed that the Michigan CIO's decision to endorse the Democrats was not a vote of approval for the party as it was then constituted. As the resolution made clear: "It is our objective in adopting this policy to remold the Democratic Party into a real liberal and progressive political party which can be subscribed to by members of the CIO and other liberals. We therefore advise CIO members to become active precinct, ward, county, and congressional district workers and to attempt to become delegates to Democratic conventions."

Open support for the Democrats was advocated for a number of reasons. In the first place, it reflected the philosophy of most of the CIO leaders that, in general, third party action was fruitless. In connection with the 1948 elections specifically, it was a move to forestall support for Henry Wallace's third-party bid for the presidency. It was equally important that at the time the Democratic Party in Michigan was virtually without leadership. Organized labor thus had an opportunity to help fill the void, gain a major voice in policy making within the party, and try to fulfill its objective of remolding the party into a "real liberal and progressive" organization.

Once the decision had been made, CIO leaders as well as some AFL adherents proceeded to forge a formal alliance with a group of liberal Michigan Democrats not identified with the labor movement, such as C. Mennen ("Soapy") Williams of Detroit and Ann Arbor's Neil Staebler. This more broadly based combination could garner wider support than could an organization composed solely of representatives of organized labor. An important AFL hold-out then and at various times since was the Teamsters union. That organization had almost succeeded in gaining control of the Democratic Party in 1948 and continued to try to do so thereafter. The Teamsters backed a candidate in opposition to Williams in the 1948 Democratic Party primaries, for example. The organization usually adhered to the coalition on the surface after 1951 but was uneasy about the lesser role it played in the coalition and in fact pursued an independent political course whenever self-interest so dictated.

The new liberal-labor alliance moved rapidly and effectively into the political arena. It managed to gain control of key delegations to the Democratic state party convention in 1948 and could thus elect its own candidate as state chairman as soon as the incumbent's term was up. More important, Soapy Williams, the coalition's candidate for the 1948 gubernatorial race, was elected as were its nominees for lieutenant-governor, attorney general and a sprinkling of candidates to the state house and U. S. Congress.

The coalition was not without opposition from old-line Democrats in the state. In fact, in the first few years of its existence, vituperation against labor's political role, in the past largely the province of the GOP, was hurled at it from within the ranks of the Democrats. "I have just seen socialism take over the Democratic Party by Communist methods," said one, while another said, "Socialists are in complete charge of the Democratic Party machinery." The liberal-labor coalition withstood the barrage, however, and by the fall of 1952 was firmly in control.

During the 1950s GOP spokesmen grew louder in their charges that organized labor had seized control of Michigan. The state, said one, was run "by a bunch of millionaires [Williams, Staebler, and the then lieutenant-governor, Philip Hart] who take orders from Walter Reuther." This was something of an exaggeration, for the labor members of the coalition were by no means always successful in pressing their case in party caucuses. Moreover, because of the nature of districting in the state, which favored the Republican-dominated rural districts, the GOP was sufficiently strong in the legislature to forestall much of the proposed legislation that labor favored. In the late 1950s, for example, the Republicans defeated labor-supported proposals to expand workmen's compensation legislation, enact a graduated income tax, institute temporary unemployment compensation, exempt food and medicine from the state sales tax, and enact a minimum wage for workers not in interstate commerce. Nonetheless, the identification of labor with the Democratic Party in Michigan was perhaps stronger during the 1950s than at any other time in the state's history. The UAW, as the numerically strongest union in the state—and particularly in the key Wayne County area—was often singled out as the dominant element in the liberal-labor alliance.

Interestingly enough, during approximately the same period the Republican Party was at least as firmly identified with the automobile manufacturers, especially the Big Three. Its guiding light through the 1940s and early 1950s was Arthur Summerfield, a very successful Flint Chevrolet dealer. He was ably assisted by other auto industry representatives, particularly from General Motors and Ford. This polarization of union versus employer, transferred to the political arena, was probably more pronounced in Michigan at that time than at any other time in the history of the United States.

The Republican Party's strong dependence upon the support of the auto manufacturers was, in fact, one factor eroding its strength in the state during the 1950s. After President Eisenhower's election in November 1952, Arthur Summerfield left the state to serve as postmaster general. The man who replaced him as the GOP's state chairman, John Feikens, was unable to rally the kind of widespread support upon which Summerfield had counted. Feikens actually had to contend with a split in party ranks. To some extent the rift was a reflection of the animosity between Taft and Eisenhower factions within the GOP, which was characteristic of Republicans nationwide. And it was also a reaction to the Democratic landslide in Michigan's 1954 off-year elections, which was probably in large measure a reaction to the 1954 recession. The Democrats' judicious use during the campaign of Charles E. Wilson's remark, which appeared to equate the unemployed with kennel dogs, also contributed to their victory. Wilson was then secretary of defense in the Eisenhower Administration and was formerly president of General Motors. His statement, with reference to unemployment problems at the time, was: "I've always liked bird dogs better than kennel-fed dogs myself—you know, one who'll get out and hunt for food rather than sit on his fanny and yell." Michigan had been especially hard-hit by the 1954 recession, so that Wilson's remark had a particularly strong impact in the state.

The split in GOP ranks also reflected a struggle between two of the automotive giants for dominance in the car market, a fight that spilled over into intraparty affairs and converted two former political allies into enemies. As one observer noted: "Ford is moving heaven and earth to place Ford cars first in the hearts and minds of the public. G.M. is mad at Ford. It is mad about Ford's giving in on the supplemental unemployment benefit deal. For years G.M. officials have been supporters of the Republican party, and had a lot more political consciousness than Ford. But within recent years Ford had taken a greater interest in state affairs. So now this business jealousy has extended over into politics. They just don't like each other. If one was for God, the other would be for the Devil." When, after a bitter convention fight, Feikens was reelected Republican state chairman, General Motors executives simply refused to contribute to party coffers. This left the GOP not only split but virtually bankrupt. Its defeat in the state in the 1956 elections was even worse than the one it had suffered two years before.

By the early 1960s the Republican Party in the state had recovered from its earlier plight and had rallied around a popular vote-getter, George Romney, much as the Democrats had grouped around Williams in the previous decade. In favoring Romney, the former president of American Motors, the GOP was still choosing a man closely identified with the auto industry—but not one of the Big Three manufacturers. Romney won the gubernatorial race in 1962 and was reelected in 1964. Williams, in the interim, had left the state to serve in the Kennedy Administration, and a split had developed in Michigan's Democratic ranks that was reminiscent of the earlier rift within the GOP. The Democratic Party's disarray contributed in large measure to the GOP's ability to recapture the state senate and split the lower house down the middle in the 1966 off-year elections.

By the time of the 1968 presidential election, it was not simply the Michigan Democrats who were suffering from disharmony. In the nation as a whole the party's traditional power bases appeared hopelessly weakened. The South was strongly inclined to the Republican candidate, Richard Nixon, or to third-party candidate George Wallace. Wallace was also showing considerable strength among blue collar workers in the North. Big city machines had failed to adjust to the changed racial composition of the constituency they sought to serve and were greatly weakened. The Vietnam issue was alienating many of the older liberals and the young.

Despite this, beginning in October 1968 there was a noticeable upswing in Democrat Hubert Humphrey's chances for election. The Humphrey upsurge is generally credited to organized labor, which marshalled its forces and almost accomplished the impossible. In Michigan alone, COPE forces registered some 690,000 voters and established a 550-man telephone detail that constantly sent out the message to vote for Humphrey. In the end an evident early interest by the blue collar workers in the Wallace candidacy was largely diverted back to the Democratic camp, and Humphrey easily carried Michigan.

In summary, then, organized labor's early, sporadic, largely ineffectual, and narrowly drawn political program has been replaced in recent years by a continuing, well-organized, broadly oriented program, which functions effectively at all levels of government. Michigan, perhaps as much as or more than any other state, well illustrates these developments.

Whether or not organized labor will be able to function as effectively in the future is hard to say. Labor has never spoken with one voice in the past, but it has, over time, moved in the same direction. Its future success in politics will depend in part upon whether or not it can continue to do so—whether or not the policy makers in the AFL-CIO, in the Alliance for Labor Action, and in the independent unions will press for common goals. Perhaps even more important is the "generation gap," which is affecting the labor movement as it is every other aspect of American society. The young—better-educated and more independent than ever before—are impatient with their elders and less ready to accept their leadership unquestioningly. Unless some sort of accommodation can be achieved, with each group willing to listen to and share policy-making powers with the other, they may lose sight of their common interests, work at cross purposes, and, between them, undo much that has been achieved thus far.

LABOR'S CONTRIBUTIONS TO THE
POLITICAL PROCESS

What are the elements that have made labor effective in the political arena? Its major contributions are three: electoral manpower, money, and votes.

Electoral Manpower

Michigan serves as an excellent example of organized labor's ability to harness manpower for political purposes. Union members heeded the 1948 message to "become active precinct, ward, county and congressional district workers, and to attempt to become delgates to Democratic conventions." They have often been the backbone of the delegations to county and state party conventions where party policy and candidates are determined.

Training COPE workers in voter registration and precinct work

They were willing to run for office on the Democratic ticket in upstate counties where that party had rarely been represented on the ballot before. And, over time, they built up sufficient support in their home areas so that their bids were sometimes successful.

Labor manpower has also been crucial in voter registration drives and get-out-the-vote campaigns. As far back as the 1945 Frankensteen mayoralty race, *The New York Times* made special note of the CIO-PAC's ability to marshall doorbell ringers, baby sitters, and chauffeurs. Due to those efforts there were more voters registered and more ballots cast in that election than ever before in the city's history.

By the 1950s almost every local in the state had its own political action committee working closely with its national's counterpart and with COPE officials. They staged rallies, sent out campaign literature, manned phones and, most important of all, contacted people personally in house-to-house canvasses. Gus Scholle, head of the Michigan AFL-CIO and the state's COPE operation, put it this way: "Doorbell ringing, that's the main thing. When I used to hear all the politicians give lip service to house-to-house work, I was just dumb enough to believe them. I found out later they didn't believe it themselves, but I decided to try it—and it paid off."

Scholle was not alone in these efforts. He and his staff worked closely with another major figure in Michigan labor political circles, the late Roy Reuther. As head of the UAW's Citizenship and Legislative Department, Reuther was in a key position in a state as auto oriented as Michigan. One measure of Reuther's effectiveness in Michigan is that he was asked to codirect the national voter registration efforts on behalf of John F. Kennedy in 1960 and to take charge of the AFL-CIO's national drive in 1962 and 1964.

It is important to note that Reuther and his staff, as well as Scholle and his, did not direct their grass-roots activities solely at the organized worker in the state. Their efforts were communitywide, an appeal to all workers to exercise their rights at the ballot box. Thus their work has had the effect of educating a broad spectrum of workers to political awareness.

Money

Organized labor's financial contributions to election campaigns are still a topic of heated debate in the halls of Congress. A classic court case in this connection, *United States* vs. *U.A.W.*, arose in Michigan in the 1950s, but the issue was a fighting one long before that.

The 1936 presidential election was hardly over before some congressmen were drafting legislation to curb political expenditures by labor unions. In a sense their work was facilitated by John L. Lewis himself. At one point, for example, the flamboyant head of the Mine Workers announced: "Everybody says I want my pound of flesh, that I gave Mr. Roosevelt $500,000 for his 1936 campaign, and I want my quid pro quo. The United Mine Workers and the CIO have paid cash on the barrel head for every piece of legislation that we have gotten. . . . I say that labor's champion has to a large extent here been a bought and paid-for proposition." Such indiscreet flaunting of raw power, however exaggerated, could not be ignored.

While corporations and banks had been legally limited in their political spending as far back as 1907, the first piece of federal legislation that attempted to limit labor's political spending was the second Federal Corrupt Practices (Hatch) Act, passed just before the 1940 presidential elections. That law was so full of loopholes, however, that it was largely ineffective. Three years later a Congress largely hostile to President Roosevelt, and by no means enamored of organized labor, attached an amendment to the War Labor Disputes (Smith-Connally) Act that effectively limited labor union contributions from general funds to the campaign coffers of any federal officeseeker. When the Smith-Connally Act, a temporary wartime measure, expired, the limitations it contained concerning contributions was made permanent in Section 304 of the Taft-Hartley Act. Taft-Hartley also broadened the limitations to include "expenditures" made by labor organizations on behalf of candidates, in addition to "contributions" to campaign funds, which had been outlawed earlier. Taft-Hartley also extended the limitations to primary elections for federal office, which had not been expressly covered earlier. None of this legislation covered strictly state and local elections, although a number of states enacted laws that placed limits on political expenditures in such cases as well.

By 1943, when Smith-Connally was passed, John L. Lewis and the CIO had come to a parting of the ways, and he had taken Labor's Non-Partisan League with him. This assumed some importance after the enactment of the Smith-Connally Act since that law, and the later Taft-Hartley legislation, covered only political expenditures made from union general funds. It did not include donations made by any voluntarily supported political action committee. This was a major reason for the creation of the CIO-PAC.

In the mid-1950s, when the GOP in Michigan was suffering from the election setbacks described earlier, the U. S. Department of Justice began an investigation of the UAW's political expenditures to determine whether or not the union was violating the legislation described above. While the Justice Department representatives asserted that their action was not politically motivated, there is some evidence that they had been approached by Republican state chairman Feikens before they began their inquiry. There is also some indication that Postmaster General Summerfield and Arizona's Senator Barry Goldwater were involved in pushing the investigation.

By the time the case against the UAW was begun, the courts had already ruled in a number of other cases dealing with the expenditure of union general funds (as against voluntarily contributed donations) for political purposes. In such key cases as *United States* vs. *CIO* (1948), *United States* vs. *Painters Local Union No. 481* (1948), and *United States* vs. *Construction and General Laborers Local Union* (1951), they had determined that it was permissible for a union to use general funds to endorse candidates in its own newspaper, as well as in paid political advertisements in more widely circulated newspapers and on the radio. Nor was it deemed illegal to assign full-time union staff members to political duties while continuing to pay their salaries.

The issue in the case of *United States* vs. *UAW* was the legality of expenditures from UAW general funds for certain telecasts in the "Meet the UAW-CIO" series in which some

Democratic candidates in the 1954 elections had been interviewed. The Justice Department charged that those telecasts amounted to an endorsement of those candidates, were thus electioneering, and were therefore illegal. The UAW contended that its presentation of the candidates was a part of its overall educational program for its members; that the telecasts were part of a continuing series that consistently dealt with current topics of interests to its members; and that therefore they could not be construed as electioneering any more than could any other program that dealt with the political campaign around election time.

The case dragged through the courts from mid-July 1955, when a federal grand jury first indicted the UAW, until November 1957, when a jury upon a remand from the U. S. Supreme Court found the union "not guilty." The effect of the decision was to whittle away still further at the restraints on organized labor's political spending. Indeed, one attorney for the Justice Department who had been directly involved in the case said that the verdict made the applicable federal legislation a "dead letter" altogether. This was probably too strong a statement, however, for the issue itself is still very much alive. As recently as the end of 1969 Congress again debated and defeated proposed legislation that would have inhibited labor's political spending.

How much does labor spend on political activity? It has been estimated that, in all, the trade union movement in this country contributed about $10 million in connection with the 1968 elections. Even if this figure does not accurately reflect total goods and services contributed by unions and union members, the total amount of expenditures by organized labor, compared to the total expenditures for the same elections—in excess of $200 million—indicate that labor's share probably did not come to more than 5 percent—or certainly not over 10 percent—of the total national outlay. Thus while labor's money is important in politics, and is often very effectively deployed, it hardly justifies the assertions that are sometimes made about it. The enormous "war chest" that labor is often said to have at its disposal simply does not exist.

Votes

Labor unions do not control a large bloc of votes that can be swung to one political party or another at the whim of their leaders. In that sense, there is no such thing as a "labor vote." Representatives of union political action committees can make a definite impact upon registration drives and in getting voters to the polls on election day. But their efforts are no guarantee that union members will vote the way the union leadership might want them to. For example, a study made of UAW members in Michigan during the 1952 presidential election campaign showed that 25 percent of those interviewed voted for Dwight Eisenhower, although their union had come out strongly for Adlai Stevenson.

Except in rare cases, however, it is generally true that American industrial workers—organized or not—have been more likely to vote Democratic than Republican. Thus by encouraging workers to register and vote, politically active unions can ordinarily increase the number of Democratic ballots cast, and therefore can fundamentally affect the size of urban pluralities for Democratic candidates. This has been an important factor in determining the outcome of many statewide elections. Michigan in the past two decades is a case in point.

Until recently, even where the Democrats swept the statewide offices—and thus, presumably, were the majority party in the state as a whole—they were by no means assured of the same kind of majority within the state legislature. This discrepancy arose because it was common to favor rural over urban areas— to take geography as well as population into account—in drawing up appropriate election districts. Since the rural areas have traditionally been Republican, it was therefore quite possible that a Democratic state administration faced a Republican-dominated legislative body. This was true in Michigan, for example, throughout the 1950s. Michigan labor had much to do with the fact that it is less likely to happen today.

Since the 1940s Gus Scholle and other union leaders in the state had been pointing out that despite the fact that the 1908 Michigan constitution specifically called for districting on the basis of population, very little had been done to correct inequities resulting from population shifts over time. The electoral districts then in force therefore did not reflect population distribution. In 1952 organized labor had been instrumental in placing a constitutional amendment on the ballot that would have forced a reapportionment to bring districts into line with population. Labor leaders argued that "people, not pine stumps, should make the law." However, their amendment had been defeated, and another, known as the "balanced legislature" amendment, had been passed instead. The latter specifically permitted geography, rather than population, to govern in connection with state senatorial districts. Representation in the state house was theoretically to remain on the basis of population, but because little had been done to correct the imbalances caused by population shifts since 1908, rural domination continued in both legislative chambers in Lansing.

In late 1959 Scholle and others decided to try again. This time they took their case to the courts. The case of *Scholle* vs. [*Secretary of State*] *Hare* is an important part of the whole fight to establish the "one man/one vote" principle, not only in Michigan but in the country as a whole.

The Scholle case focused upon the senatorial districting approved by the voters in 1952. The main argument was that the amendment denied Scholle the equal protection of the law required under the 14th amendment of the U. S. Constitution. Using 1960 Census figures it was contended that Scholle's vote, as a resident of a heavily populated district in the Detroit area, was worth only one thirteenth that of a voter living in the most overrepresented district in Michigan. By 1970 it was estimated his vote would probably be worth only one twenty-fifth.

The case was first argued before the Michigan Supreme Court in 1960. That body, relying on earlier U. S. Supreme Court decisions, decided against Scholle on the grounds that malapportionment was a "political" rather than a "legal" matter. Scholle immediately filed an appeal to the U. S. Supreme Court. Before that body heard the appeal (in late April of 1962), it had issued its opinion in *Baker* vs. *Carr*. In the latter case the court reversed its earlier position that apportionment questions were "political" and held that they were, instead, subject to judicial scrutiny. Thus when the Scholle case came before it, the U. S. Supreme Court sent the case back to the

Michigan court to be reexamined in the light of its revised policy. When the state high court reviewed the case, it, too, reversed itself. Its decision, handed down in July 1962, became the first in the country to hand down the "one man/one vote" principle. The decision was widely regarded as a personal victory for Scholle and a triumph for organized labor in the state since much of the nonlabor element in Michigan's Democratic Party was slow to support Scholle's action; and it was the AFL-CIO alone that footed the bill for the legal expenses.

The Michigan Supreme Court's ruling caused much consternation among those who opposed it, and they were quick to label the justices as "dupes of the AFL-CIO." The opposition immediately started legal counterproceedings to invalidate the decision and thereby threw Michigan's electoral processes into a state of chaos. The adoption of a new state constitution in 1963, which set forth yet another method of determining senatorial districts (80 percent on population, 20 percent on geography) added further to the confusion and resulted in even more legal action and counteraction.

After the U. S. Supreme Court handed down its 1964 decision in *Reynolds* vs. *Sims,* which definitely accepted the standard of one man/one vote, the Michigan Supreme Court ordered the state legislature immediately to redraw the senatorial districts in accordance with that decision. When the legislative commission assigned to that task deadlocked, the court itself ordered the adoption of the so-called Kleiner-Austin plan, which was generally conceded to be the most equitable for redividing the state on a population basis. Because of the court's swift action, Michigan became the first state in the nation to redistrict in accordance with the Reynolds decision. Redistricting was accomplished in time for the 1964 elections. As a result (although also due to the impact of the Democratic landslide against GOP presidential candidate Goldwater) those elections gave the Democrats control of both legislative chambers in Lansing for the first time since the 1932 Roosevelt landslide.

Opposition to the one man/one vote concept was not limited to Michigan alone. After the Supreme Court decision in the Reynolds case, antireapportionment forces in the U. S. Congress, led by Senator Everett Dirksen, tried delaying tactics, which would have prevented judicial consideration of reapportionment cases for from two to four years. Their hope was that, in the interim, state legislatures would ratify a constitutional amendment that would nullify the Supreme Court's decision. Organized labor jumped in quickly and forcefully to defeat that attempt. It was the first and most important interest group in the country to do so.

Thus while organized labor may not be able to dictate how a man votes, it has played a major role in assuring that his vote, whatever it may be, counts as much as that of anyone else.

IN RETROSPECT

What has all the expenditure in time, energy, and money in the political arena accomplished in Michigan? Labor's efforts were clearly important in making Michigan a two-party state. Moreover, its active role in party policy-making helped to mold the state's Democratic Party into something like the "liberal and progressive" organization of which the 1948 CIO convention delegates had dreamed.

Michigan labor's impact has been wider yet. As one of the prominent liberals in the original liberal-labor alliance commented recently, labor's representatives "opened up frozen minds," not solely within the Democratic Party but in the opposition camp as well. Increasingly, labor's political participation has acquired a substantial degree of legitimacy. The loud cries against a labor "takeover" have long since diminished to a mere whisper.

Its wide-ranging publicity campaigns served an important educational function in the state. Neil Staebler, one of the leaders in the original liberal-labor coalition, stated recently that he considers this "one of the most important things labor has done politically." He went on to explain:

> Through union papers and the TV and radio shows which it then sponsored, labor kept up a drumfire of publicity about legislative issues, candidates, party politics, and public problems. In many outlying areas of the State, where newspapers pay very little attention to state and national politics, labor news greatly stepped up the awareness of

labor people and, through them, spread a modicum of information more widely in the public. In the metropolitan areas, the papers go through cycles of objectivity and indifference, paying little attention to some problems and subjects for long periods of time and tending to give much more attention to Republican candidates close to election time. Labor news has served a great purpose here in filling gaps. It may also have served a great long-term function in prodding the media to do a more balanced job of treating the news and a more complete job of paying attention to governmental and political affairs.

Because the Michigan legislature was dominated by rural interests for so long a time, much of labor's lobbying and legislative efforts were directed toward holding off unfavorable labor legislation and toward modernizing worker-protective legislation. In recent years organized labor and its sympathizers, with substantial support from GOP governor George Romney, have succeeded in liberalizing the state's workmen's compensation and unemployment benefits legislation to the extent that these social welfare programs are among the more progressive in the country.

Beyond these efforts of immediate concern to workers, labor has also pushed for a whole range of legislation of wider public benefit. Included within such types of legislation are substantial efforts to broaden free educational opportunities throughout the state and to develop inexpensive higher educational opportunities for all young people. Mental health programs and mental hospitals have been substantially improved, though much remains to be done. Civil rights programs and equal opportunities legislation have been enacted, and the administrative and enforcement programs adopted to implement them are in the vanguard of such state efforts in the nation.

Labor has pushed for a rational highway expansion and modernization program and has joined with conservation forces in seeking extensive funds for natural resources preservation and for the development of a statewide system of parks. These are much needed if urban workers are to enjoy the benefits of what still remains of a once-great wilderness preserve.

Finally, labor has moved strongly to protect its right to bargain and to strike and has sought to expand collective bargaining privileges to groups of workers who could traditionally not avail themselves of them. The Michigan Public Employment Relations Act of 1965, which provides representation and collective bargaining rights to a wide variety of public employees in the state, is one of the most thoroughgoing of such pieces of legislation thus far enacted anywhere in the United States.

Organized labor in Michigan, as elsewhere in the country, has contributed to the increasing democratization of American society. It broadens the base of the electorate; it informs those to whom it speaks about major public policy programs of the times; and it encourages workers to participate in politics. Each of these efforts tends to make the average citizen's participation in politics more meaningful and creative.

7

UNIONISM GOES PUBLIC

During the past decade public employee unionization has emerged as the most important development in the area of labor-management relations in the country. It is a rare day indeed when the newspapers and evening news telecasts fail to report some item such as "Warren Teachers on Strike!"; "San Francisco Municipal Employees Tie Up City!"; or "Blue Flu in Livonia." Garbage collectors strike in North Carolina, teaching fellows refuse to meet their classes in Ann Arbor, policemen sit in in Milwaukee, firemen stay home in Lansing, and letter carriers let the mail pile up in New York City. Just as one group ends its walk-out, another hits the bricks. And so it continues with no end in sight.

In recent years labor organizations in the public sector have accounted for more than half the total growth in union membership in the United States. Moreover, the rate of growth has been accelerating: between 1966 and 1968 public employee organizations gained members at four times the rate of the union movement as a whole.

The extraordinary growth in unions is only one aspect of the phenomenal change that has taken place in public sector labor relations. A decade ago, a signed written agreement between a public employee union and a governmental unit was a rarity. Today it is commonplace. To illustrate this change, in 1942 a handful of Michigan municipalities had signed agreements with unions representing groups of their workers. Over 20 years later, in 1964, the situation had not changed markedly: only about 10 percent of them had such agreements. Yet, only five years later, in 1969, over 70 percent of the towns with 4000 inhabitants or more had them. It is this kind of explosion in public sector unionism that has led to it being called a revolution.

Public employees are latecomers to collective bargaining primarily because they were specifically excluded from the labor legislation enacted in the 1930s that encouraged collective bargaining in the private sector. That purposeful exclusion was grounded in the theory that the collective bargaining process was unsuited to government personnel. Governmental sovereignty could not be challenged, nor could public decision-making power be delegated to private organizations. As President Franklin D. Roosevelt explained in 1937: "The very nature and purposes of government make it impossible for administrative officials to represent fully or to bind the employer in mutual discussions with public employee organizations. The employer is the whole people, who speak by means of laws enacted by their representatives. ... Accordingly, administrative officials and employees alike are governed and guided, and in many cases restricted, by laws which establish policies, procedures and rules in personnel matters." Even as strong an advocate of trade unionism as Samuel Gompers did not question the fact that public employees could not engage in collective bargaining. One reason he opposed the nationalization of railroads and mines in this country was that he was sure that it would spell the end of unions in those industries.

It was widely argued that government employees received benefits that offset the denial of collective bargaining rights. They had greater job security than did employees in the private sector. A substantial number were covered by civil service regulations designed to protect them from unfair or arbitrary treatment. Moreover, they received fringe benefits—paid sick leaves and vacations, pensions, shorter workweeks—that were less prevalent and of more limited scope and value in the private sector. Such fringes, it was felt, compensated for the public servant's basic wage or salary scale which was often lower than that of a comparable job in the private sector.

Government employees themselves were ordinarily uninterested in joining a union in any event. Many of them held semiprofessional or professional white collar positions and thought of their jobs as being different from those held by blue collar workers in private industry.* Moreover, civil service regulations called for a promotion system based on individual merit, which tended to heighten competition among the members of any given work group. In that sense, the employment situation did differ from that in a unionized shop where promotion was often governed by straight seniority. To put it another way, the public servant viewed his promotion as a reward; the trade unionist thought of his as a right.

The public sector was thus harder to organize. Moreover, government employees represented only a small proportion of the total civilian labor force—about 6 percent in 1930 for example. With so much organizational work to be done among industrial workers, and so many more of them, trade unions tended to concentrate their efforts on that group and to overlook the government worker.

Public employees generally did have a legal right to organize. However, the courts usually held that government managers could not recognize or bargain with unions. Furthermore, in some jurisdictions, organizaton was followed by reprisals against those who had joined the union. Thus, the collective bargaining route was largely closed, although there were exceptions. Some public employers recognized and bargained with labor organizations. A notable example at the federal level was the Tennessee Valley Authority (TVA), which granted its employ-

* The difference in job perception applied equally to white collar workers in the private sector. Although that group of workers is not specifically covered in this chapter, they, too, are now joining unions to a greater degree than in the past, and for many of the same reasons as are public employees.

ees the right to organize and bargain through representatives of their own choosing as early as 1935 and signed its first written labor contract in 1940. At the local level, some of the larger cities, such as Detroit, Cincinnati. and Philadelphia had some form of collective bargaining with city employees going back many years. Nonetheless, these were isolated cases, and flew in the face of prevailing theory and sentiment.

While public employee organizations usually did not engage in collective bargaining, they could and did use the political route to gain their ends. In time they developed some of the strongest lobbies to come before Congress and the individual state legislatures. Postal employees, who were spread evenly across the country, and could thus speak to all congressmen with an equally effective voice, were especially noted for their lobbying successes.

Resort to strike action by government employees was almost universally condemned. A walkout by the Boston police in 1919 evoked the celebrated remark by the then governor of Massachusetts, Calvin Coolidge, that "There is no right to strike against the public safety by anybody, anywhere, at any time." President Franklin Roosevelt called any public employee strike "unthinkable and intolerable," since such action looked toward "the paralysis of government by those sworn to uphold it." A Michigan official called them "a form of rebellion against the government," and went on to say, "To permit public employees to exercise such power is to deny the sovereignty of government itself and to substitute government by coercion, fear and favor, rather than government by law." The law agreed. Traditionally, public employee strikes were held to be illegal under common law. During the 1940s the federal government bolstered the common law doctrine by enacting legislation that specifically prohibited such strikes. So did a number of states—Michigan, with its 1947 Hutchinson Act, among them. Such legislation usually called for some sort of punitive action against strikers. The Michigan statute, for example, called for automatic discharge.

Such legal obstacles did not altogether prevent public employee strikes, however. In Michigan, for instance, there were a scattering of them in the nineteenth century: a walkout of

Detroit sewer workers in 1885 and a strike by construction and maintenance employees in the same city's waterworks in 1894. During the latter, a battle erupted between the county sheriff and his men and some of the strikers. Three strikers were killed, and another twelve people, including the sheriff and a deputy, seriously injured.

In the first decades of the twentieth century, there were other stoppages. One of the most unusual took place in Ypsilanti, in 1921, when all of the town's firemen walked out in an attempt to secure a raise for their chief. That strike failed, making it impossible to say what, if anything, the chief might have done for his men in return.

The greatest number of walkouts by government workers before the recent explosion were bunched in the early 1930s and were particularly frequent among workers on WPA projects. Even that outcropping, however, was mild compared to the events of recent years.

WHY THE "REVOLUTION"?

The new-found militancy among public employees has its roots in a number of changes that have taken place in the last 15 or 20 years. For one thing, the traditional advantages of public over private employment—job security, fringe benefits, and the like—became less marked after World War II when the same benefits became increasingly available to workers in the private sector. Furthermore, the gap between wage and salary scales in the public service and those in the private sector widened still further. Teachers, for example, became increasingly aware that their salaries were commonly far below those paid for positions in industry that required the same amount of education and training.

While the creation of civil service commissions around the country had done much to end the spoils system, those same commissions came to represent simply another aspect of the management personnel function to the public employee once the initial fervor for "good government" died down. As one U. S. senator noted, in describing the U. S. Civil Service Commission: "A lot of the bloom has been worn off the idealistic rose ... [and] the Civil Service Commission has proved itself, particularly in recent years, and particularly its top management, to be management-oriented to the point of prejudice, a mere subjunct to the Bureau of the Budget, and no more representative of the aims, needs, desires and aspirations of the rank-and-file federal employee than is the National Association of Manufacturers." There were complaints that favoritism had crept in in connection with promotions. Other critics contended that individual merit meant little in a large bureaucratic setting and that seniority governed instead. (Beyond this, of course, not all public servants came under civil service regulations in any event.)

Lobbying had its drawbacks as well. Even the postal employees, who had traditionally been such an effective pressure group, found, for a variety of reasons, that their lobbying had become less successful.

Thus, as the traditional advantages to public employment eroded, the disadvantages multiplied. Public employees came to feel that they were being treated as second-class citizens in American society. This was a major factor in making them more receptive to the idea of joining a union.

At the same time, organized labor could no longer afford to overlook the public sector. In recent years, government—particularly state and local—has become the fastest growing "industry" in the country. Public employees now represent about 16 percent of the civilian labor force, and estimates indicate that by 1975 they will account for at least 20 percent. Some traditional labor organizations, such as the Machinists and Teamsters, which formerly concentrated their efforts on the private sector, therefore began giving substantial attention to organizational drives among government employees, in terms of both time and money.

Moreover, once the government began encouraging collective bargaining in the private sector, it became increasingly difficult to try to justify its position with regard to the public employee. As a 1955 American Bar Association committee reported: "A government which imposes upon private employers certain obligations in dealing with their employees may not in good faith refuse to deal with its own public servants on a reasonably similar basis,. modified, of course, to meet the exigencies of public service."

The country's high rate of employment also had a substantial impact. Because of the tight labor market during most of the 1950s and 1960s, public managers were less willing to apply punitive measures legally available to them against striking employees. As a member of the Michigan mediation service commented in connection with an Ecorse teachers strike, "It's kind of a futile gesture to fire 194 teachers when you can't even find 10 to replace them." Once it became clear that strike action brought results, the number of walkouts multiplied. If it worked for one group, would it not work for another? During the March 1970 postal strike, a New York City mailman told a reporter, "Everybody else strikes and gets a big pay increase. The teachers, sanitation men and transit workers all struck in violation of the law and got big increases. Why shouldn't we? We've been nice guys too long."

THE FEDERAL PROGRAM

The first significant breakthrough in public sector labor relations at the national level was President John F. Kennedy's Executive Order 10988, issued in January of 1962. (An important forerunner to that order was Mayor Robert F. Wagner's executive order of March 31, 1958, which set forth positive guidelines governing collective bargaining between New York City officials and city employees.) Executive Order 10988 for the first time established as general policy that employees in the federal service had the right to organize and bargain collectively through representatives of their own choosing.

The 1962 Executive Order did not, however, give federal employees the same rights accorded to workers in the private sector. This continues to be true under Executive Order 11491, President Nixon's 1969 revision of the earlier order. Strikes are prohibited, and bargainable issues are limited. Both orders contain the requirement that any agreement reached must contain a strong "management rights" clause, which specifically states that management representatives retain the right to hire, promote, transfer, assign and direct, suspend, demote, discipline, and discharge employees under their supervision.

A number of other major issues, such as salaries, length of the basic work day, number of holidays, basic vacation entitlement, pensions and insurance benefits also fall outside the scope of collective bargaining in the federal service since they are unilaterally established by the Congress.

Despite these limitations, collective bargaining agreements at the federal level are of steadily increasing consequence, particularly as unions succeed in negotiating the right to have a voice in matters formerly regarded as strictly "management prerogatives."

Perhaps of greatest importance, most of the agreements that have been negotiated provide for a grievance procedure with the right to appeal the decision before a neutral outsider. Under President Kennedy's order, such appeals ordinarily culminated in advisory arbitration. The 1969 order, however, moves closer to binding arbitration since agencies can no longer reject adverse awards, and only rarely will they be able successfully to appeal them.

The impact of the new program on federal employee organization has been considerable. By the end of 1968, only six years after President Kennedy issued that first order, more than half of all eligible federal employees were in exclusive bargaining units.

THE MICHIGAN EXPERIENCE

The Kennedy Executive Order acted as a spur to other governmental units and was one factor in changing state and local employee relations policies. Another equally important factor was reapportionment—the redrawing of electoral districts to reflect the one man/one vote principle. As state legislatures were affected by redistricting, they came to reflect a stronger urban orientation than they formerly had. Consequently, there was less hostility to the principle of unionization and more sympathy toward the idea of granting some form of collective bargaining rights to state and local employees. For example, the Michigan Legislature enacted a revision of the 1947 Hutchinson Act, the Public Employment Relations Act (PERA), in 1965—the year after the state was reapportioned. Michigan was one of 11 states to pass such legislation that year and the next.

By 1969, 30 states had enacted some form of legislation that permitted public employee bargaining. (The state acts, it should be noted, are by no means uniform although almost all of them prohibit public employee strikes, and most provide some alternate means of dispute settlement.)

The Michigan act has been described as a combination of the earlier Hutchinson Act and the federal government's Wagner Act. PERA reflects the former in that strikes are still prohibited. However, the Hutchinson Act's automatic discharge penalty has been softened, so that disciplinary measures are now in graduated steps, up to and including dismissal. They may also be appealed in the appropriate circuit court. The 1965 legislation is like the Wagner Act in that it accords public employees the right to bargain collectively through representatives of their own choosing. It transforms the Michigan Labor Mediation Board* (since renamed the Employment Relations Commission) into a miniature NLRB, which has the authority to hold elections and certify bargaining units and agents. Such units are to be on the principle of exclusive representation. The employer is obligated to bargain in good faith with the certified representative. If he fails to do so, an unfair labor practice charge can be filed against him with the commission.

Michigan was not the first state to pass legislation protecting the right of public employees to bargain collectively. That fell to Wisconsin. Michigan's 1965 law is, however, among the strongest of the state acts in terms of the rights it gives to unionized government employees coming under the scope of the act. Moreover, there is probably no state where enactment of such legislation had such immediate and far-reaching results. According to Robert Howlett, chairman of the Employment Relations Commission, the passage of PERA caused "a nuclear explosion." As soon as it was passed, "public employees rushed their representation petitions to the Labor Mediation Board [as the commission was then still called], which had neither

---

* The three-member board was originally established in 1939 to provide for fact-finding, mediation and arbitration of labor disputes in the private sector in Michigan with specific reference to hospital and public utility workers. The 1947 Hutchinson Act added public employee disputes to the board's duties, although such cases could not go to arbitration.

personnel nor office space nor paper clips to administer the new law." During the first two years following the passage of PERA, the commission received over 800 certification petitions and some 175 unfair labor practice charges. In all, something like 1500 labor agreements were signed just in the first two years the act was in force.

At the present time, the vast majority of the state's primary and secondary school teachers are organized, and faculty at the state's colleges and universities are also beginning to show some interest in unionism, particularly at the junior college level. The administration at Central Michigan University was the first at a four-year college anywhere in the country to enter into a collectively-bargained wage agreement with its faculty. Among the nonacademic employees at public institutions of higher learning in Michigan, all service and maintenance personnel are organized and working under contract. The bulk of the police and firemen in the state are unionized as are a good number of Michigan's county and township employees. As indicated earlier, municipal employees are heavily organized. A number of public employee unions have been granted dues check-off, a few have union shop agreements, and many more operate under the agency shop principle (Under an agency shop agreement, all employees in the bargaining unit must either join the union or tender fees—usually equal to the amount of union dues—for services they receive from their bargaining agent.)

Employees in classified state civil service positions are not covered by PERA because the 1963 Constitution prohibits the state legislature from enacting laws that would apply to them. Nonetheless, a fair number of them are union members, and written labor agreements with individual state agencies are not uncommon. Moreover, the state Civil Service Commission has recently moved to give those employees a greater voice in discussions concerning wages, hours and working conditions.

A number of unions are organizing public employees. Some, like the American Federation of Government Employees and the National Association of Government Employees, draw their membership solely from among federal employees. The American Federation of State, County and Municipal Employees, as its name implies, recruits only public servants at those levels of government. Other organizations, such as the International Association of Firefighters and the National Association of Letter Carriers, limit their membership to particular kinds of government service. While most of the organizing in Michigan, as elsewhere, has been done by unions that devote their efforts exclusively to the public sector, the trade unions that have traditionally drawn their strength from the private sector have also been active. The Teamsters, for example, have organized school bus drivers, city truck drivers and equipment operators, and some police units. The building trades unions are often the bargaining agent for craftsmen in government service, while the United Mine Workers currently represent some groups of school employees in the Upper Peninsula.

THE TEACHERS

Among the most militant groups of employees in the public sector throughout the country are the primary and secondary level teachers. One of the major reasons for this is the well-publicized competition between the state and local affiliates of **the American Federation of Teachers (AFT)**, the AFL-CIO teachers union, and those of the National Education Association (NEA). The NEA was formerly purely a professional organization, but in recent years it has taken on a new image. In doing so, the NEA is a leading example of one of the major developments in public employee unionism. Many former professional associations, still often refusing to characterize themselves as unions, nevertheless qualify for recognition as their members' bargaining agent and negotiate collective agreements just as do traditional unions.

The competition between the AFT and NEA is analogous to the rivalry between the AFL and CIO during the 1930s and 1940s. There is some indication that the two teacher organizations, like the AFL and CIO, will eventually merge, although in a somewhat different fashion. The AFL-CIO combined first at the national level and thereafter at the lower levels. The AFT and NEA, on the other hand, are coming together at the local level, while the parent organizations continue to remain separate. The first merger of local AFT and NEA affiliates in the country occurred in Flint in October 1969. Since then, others, such as the local units in Los Angeles, have combined, and still more are actively discussing the possibility of a merger.

Unionism among teachers has had a significant impact on the conditions under which they work. As a result of the negotiations over the past few years, their salaries and other compensation levels have improved dramatically. In Michigan, for instance, teachers' salaries have risen by about 40 percent in just four years.

PROBLEMS OF PUBLIC EMPLOYEE BARGAINING

Public employee bargaining in Michigan faces many of the same limitations that were described relative to the federal level. Civil service laws, teacher tenure acts, and pension and

Detroit teachers' picket line during the 1967 strike

retirement statutes have been construed as placing limits on the issues that are open to labor-management discussion.

Diffusion of Decison-Making Power

The union negotiator also faces a diffusion of decision-making authority uncommon in the private sector. Management negotiators for individual companies usually have broad discretion to commit their organizations on almost all matters. This is frequently not the case in the public sector. A government agency head may be restricted on the issues he is empowered to negotiate. Even the chief executive often does not have final say on the distribution of funds. Instead, he may only have the power to make recommendations to a legislative body.

There is a diversity of authority between local and state government, between executive and legislative branch, and within the executive branch itself. The description given by the personnel director of the Philadelphia Civil Service Commission applies equally well to many a Michigan situation: "consider the confusion of responsbility for action or determination in the conduct of negotiations in Philadelphia. Any other public jurisdiction will present an almost similar picture. Involved are the Mayor, Personnel Director, Managing Director, Finance Director, City Council—and its appropriations and finance committees, and the Civil Service Commission. Each City official and every City body mentioned has prerogatives which must be recognized and considered by everyone else in the act."

Where the legislative body is the final arbiter, "end run" or "double deck" bargaining may take place. That is, the union turns to lobbying in an effort to pressure the legislators into granting those demands it could not secure at the bargaining table. In such cases, collective bargaining is merely an indecisive and preliminary skirmish. The final battle takes place before the legislators.

Setting the Bargaining Unit

The way in which a particular bargaining unit is drawn often determines what the bargainable issues will be. This occurs because in the public sector the union generally is permitted to bargain only over issues within the authority of the manager of the particular unit for which it serves as agent, not with the head of the agency to which that unit belongs. To give an extreme example, if the certified bargaining unit were to include only the members of a particular stenographic pool, the union's "opposite number" would be the stenographers' supervisor. Needless to say, the number of issues over which such a supervisor has discretionary power, and therefore authority to bargain, would be rather limited. Thus, the determination of the appropriate bargaining unit assumes much greater importance in the public sector than in the private.

In addition, in government there has been a tendency to classify as "supervisor" many employees whose range of responsibilities are small and who would not fall into the management group in a comparable private sector setting. One union leader recently contended that in the federal service the term "supervisor" has been defined so broadly "that it is almost literally true that an employee 'supervising' one wastebasket has been termed a 'supervisor.' " This becomes important where supervisors are legally excluded from membership in a bargaining unit that also includes employees whom they supervise, as is generally the case. Some governmental jurisdictions do include at least some levels of supervision within collective bargaining units and, given the broad way in which "supervisor" is defined, there may be some logic in doing so.

Impasse Settlement

One question that is frequently raised is whether or not the distinction now made between public and private sector employees is really valid. Currently, for example, employees of a privately owned city transit company have the right to strike; their counterparts in a municipally owned company ordinarily do not. Yet, the potential inconvenience to the public is precisely the same. Thus, some students of the American labor scene are asking whether other criteria should be set up to determine under what circumstances strikes should be prohibited. There are those who argue that strikes that would endanger the public health or safety should be prohibited regardless of whether or not they originate in the private or public sector. Any other walkout, they feel, should be legal—again regardless of sector.

Even if the laws were to be changed, there would in all likelihood still be some workers who would be forbidden to strike. This raises another question: What alternate remedies should be available to them? What should they get instead? As one observer noted, in reporting the Montreal police strike, "Society cannot legislate against strikes among civil servants unless it is prepared to guarantee that they will have no cause to feel aggrieved."

What machinery should be developed to ensure that this group of public servants are treated fairly? One possibility is compulsory arbitration. This remedy is now available in Michigan and Pennsylvania with regard to deadlocked contract disputes involving police and firemen in the state. If a deadlock develops and cannot be settled satisfactorily within 30 days by means of mediation or fact-finding, either party to a Michigan dispute may request arbitration. The award rendered is binding on the parties and enforceable through court action. The legislation that established this procedure for Michigan's police and firemen is a trial balloon. It went into effect in October 1969 and runs only until the end of June 1972. Its renewal will depend upon how well it has worked or what other alternatives have developed in the meantime.

Another possible solution to the question of strike prohibition is also evolving in Michigan and some other states—this time by means of judicial decision rather than legislative action. The Michigan courts have ruled that while public employees can be enjoined from striking, an injunction will not be issued automatically against every such strike as soon as it begins. Instead, the granting of such an injunction is subject to traditional equity considerations. That is, the struck employer must make a clear showing that he acted justly in dealing with his employees and is not in part responsible for bringing on the strike. ("He who asks equity must have done equity.") The employer must also show that if the strike were allowed to continue it would cause "violence, irreparable injury, or breach of peace," and that, therefore, a civil suit against the union for money damages would be inadequate. The application of these standards gives both parties a kind of rough justice and, additionally, gives the public a reasonable degree of protection.

Union Security

Judicial decisions may well determine the answers to other problems unique to public sector relations. For example, cases involving the problem of union security are being brought before the state courts in Michigan. In some of these the issue is simply whether a union shop or an agency shop is appropriate in the public sector. President Nixon's Executive Order 11491 states flatly that union security clauses are not permissible in the federal service. While federal policy need not influence what the Michigan courts decide, it will almost certainly be used as an argument by those opposed to such clauses. Thus far, however, the state courts have upheld the agency shop provisions.

Some of the cases coming before the courts are more complicated in that teacher tenure legislation is also involved. In the typical situation, a school board has signed an agency shop agreement and individual teachers, with tenure, have refused either to join the union or to pay the alternate fee required of non-members. Those teachers have then been dismissed at the end of the school year for their refusal and have, in turn, appealed that action on the ground that their employment was secure under the state's teacher tenure legislation. Lately, such cases (and a similar group action in Detroit) have had the backing of the "Michigan Citizens for Right to Work," a latter-day open shop movement. The Michigan group is supported by a national organization, the National Right to Work Committee, formed in 1955 for the express purpose of combatting "compulsory unionism." The organization's first president was Fred Hartley, coauthor of the Taft-Hartley Act. Since it was formed, it has backed successful efforts to enact right-to-work legislation in 19 states and has pressured for the prohibition of union security clauses in public sector contracts generally. The committee also actively opposes organizing drives among agricultural workers and has supported recent congressional efforts to limit union political spending.

It is too early to tell how effective the committee's efforts will be on behalf of the protesting Michigan teachers. Nonetheless, the historical echo continues: Wherever organized labor may wander, the open shop advocates are never far behind.

Money

A fundamental problem in public sector bargaining is that it runs into the requirements and limitations involving financial and budgetary procedure. Budget deadlines, taxing power, and income aids from state and federal sources all come into play. For example, school boards often do not know how much money will be allocated to them until quite late in the fiscal year, after schools have closed for the summer. Yet, if they are to be assured of an adequate teaching force, they must be prepared to make some sort of estimate regarding salaries before their teachers scatter for the summer.

Union negotiators complain that management first tells them that negotiations on money matters are impossible because budgets have not yet been set and later turns around and tells them that such negotiations are impossible because they have. Often the public employer is equally frustrated because he is, in fact, hemmed in by limitations on power or funds. In a sense, in many bargaining relationships, labor and management are actually negotiating with the public itself for funds.

The availability of money surpasses all other problems connected with public sector bargaining. To a large extent, of course, this is also true in the private sector. The difference is that, in the private sector, the decision to grant or deny union demands is an economic one, based on the profit motive. In the public sector, on the other hand, the decision is primarily a political one. Normally, the officials charged with control and determination of budget and tax rates are elected. They are, therefore, very responsive to public opinion and thus reluctant to raise taxes. At the same time, if they are faced with a possible strike or slowdown, they must try to decide which will cause the least public outcry—the cessation or cutback in services or a tax hike. Increasingly, they are blocked in both directions. Their constituents insist upon the public services they are accustomed to but often balk at the idea of paying more to support them.

The problem of finding new revenue sources is most acute at the local level. In general, there are three major sources available to finance government: sales taxes, income taxes, and property taxes. However, as is true in Michigan, local governments in this country—municipalities, counties, and school districts—often have no authority to levy sales taxes. Moreover, state legislatures frequently limit the amount of tax that its local units may impose. In Michigan, the ceiling is a flat 1 percent for residents and .5 percent for commuters, and, as is common throughout the country, the imposition of a local income tax can be vetoed by the voters—a route rarely open to the American taxpayer in connection with state or federal levies. Thus, in the end, the property tax is the workhorse of local government and accounts for 90 percent of all local tax revenue throughout the United States. Yet, in Michigan as elsewhere, the amount of millage that can be levied upon property without authorization of the voters is specified by law.

The local Michigan official, then, is faced with PERA—a state-imposed obligation to negotiate wages and fringe benefits— which inevitably means increased expenditures for employee compensation. At the same time, he must deal with the state-imposed limitations upon unilateral taxing power and a constituency already critical of its tax burden and reluctant to give its consent to taxing itself still more.

An example that highlights the problem occurred in Detroit in 1967. Following both a "ticket-writing strike" and a "blue flu" epidemic among police officers, the parties finally referred the issue of police salaries to a neutral three-member panel. The panel recommended that the police officers' salaries be raised substantially. Money to pay the recommended increases could be found on an emergency basis within Detroit's operating budget that year, but after the first year, the panel concluded that "the City of Detroit urgently needs new taxing authority which can be granted only by the State Legislature ... Detroit is in serious financial trouble, and we join others who have suggested that the State Legislature raise the authorized level of the municipal income tax, ... restore the authority to levy local excise [sales] taxes, and ... revise the 2 percent restriction on property tax levels.*

The problem of financial straight-jacketing in the face of

---

* The Legislature has since authorized Detroit to raise its income tax on residents to 2 percent. Commuters still pay only .5 percent. Detroit is the only Michigan municipality which has been authorized to raise its tax on local residents' income above 1 percent.

collective bargaining pressure is equally serious for school districts. As stated earlier, the salaries of Michigan teachers have increased by about 40 percent in the last four years. Most, if not all, of these increases were long overdue, but they resulted in severe pressure on school district budgets. By the 1967–68 academic year—the second full year of collective bargaining under PERA—school administrators were finding it necessary to liquidate operating reserves, dip into money set aside for buildings and site expansion, or cut back program, in order to cover the salary increases. Most important, although Michigan law is generally construed to forbid school districts from deficit financing, a quarter of those studied in one survey were operating in the red by the end of fiscal 1968.

While financial constraints are most severe at the local level, every level of government is faced with them to some degree, and thus far no satisfactory solution has been found to deal with them. At some point, however, an equitable balance will have to be achieved, which safeguards the rights both of the public servant and of those whom he seeks to serve.

If the money problem and the others raised by public employee unionization can be resolved, the solutions arrived at may well have applications relevant to labor-management relations generally. Thus far, the transfer of ideas has been all one way: from the private sector to the public. In the future, a fruitful exchange may develop. Clearly, the differences between the two are not as great as was once commonly thought.

THE IMPACT OF PUBLIC EMPLOYEE UNIONISM

The coming of collective bargaining to the public sector is the most significant development in the industrial relations field in the last decade. It has obvious implications for those in government service, as well as for citizens generally. It has already had an important effect on the labor movement in the nation. During the latter part of the 1950s, trade union membership in the United States did not keep pace with the growth in the labor force. This was due largely to the relative decline in employment in the industries where unions had been strongest and to the failure of the labor movement to appeal to the growing technical and white collar segment of the labor force.

Another reason for the decline was the belief held by many young people that the labor movement was simply another self-seeking pressure group.

The coming of trade unionism and unionlike behavior to the public sector has begun to change all of this. Government alone has provided enough new recruits to the labor movement to reverse the decline in trade union membership. The government employees who join unions could conceivably change the image of the labor movement as well, particularly as white collar organizational successes in the public sector make unionism acceptable to white collar workers and technicians in private industry. The fact that teachers are engaging in collective bargaining could well have an impact upon the next generation of Americans. The young people see their teachers joining unions, engaging in collective bargaining, and signing agreements in the normal course of events. Occasionally, they even see their teachers participating in strikes or other forms of concerted action. Will this not change the image of the labor movement for the next generation?

In summary, as one watches the story of public employee unionism unfold, it is clear that there are many parallels between its development and the past history of labor organization in the private sector. In many ways, the public employee "revolution" is just another step in the direction of giving all American workers the rights and benefits that were once the privileges of a very few.

SOME SIGNIFICANT DATES IN MICHIGAN LABOR HISTORY

1818 — The Detroit Mechanics' Society established
1830 — The Ypsilanti Workingmen's Society formed
1837 — Detroit journeymen carpenters struck for higher wages and shorter hours
1838 — Detroit journeymen cordwainers opened up their own shoestore
    — Marshall Mechanics' Association formed
1839 — Detroit printers published the *Rat Gazette,* the first labor paper in the state
1852 — Detroit printers joined the International Typographical Union
1863 — The Brotherhood of Locomotive Engineers formally established, in Detroit
1864 — The Detroit Trades Assembly, the first city central body in Michigan, formed, with Richard Trevellick as its first president
1866 — The National Labor Union organized
1868 — Interest in the eight-hour day movement at its height, and first federal eight-hour legislation enacted
1869 — The Knights of Labor organized
1878 — The first Knights of Labor assembly in Michigan formed, in Detroit
    — The peak year for the Greenback-Labor Party
1880 — The Detroit Council of Trades and Labor Unions established
1883 — The Michigan Bureau of Labor and Industrial Statistics created
1885 — The workers in the Saginaw Valley lumber mills and salt blocks struck against their employers for a ten-hour day
1886 — The American Federation of Labor organized. Samuel Gompers named the AFL's first president, and held that post every year but one (1895) until his death
1889 — The Michigan Federation of Labor formed, and Joseph Labadie named its first president
1901 — The open shop movement launched
1913-14 — The Western Federation of Miners struck the Copper Country mineowners
1924 — AFL President Samuel Gompers died; succeeded by William Green
1933 — National Industrial Recovery Act passed
1935 — Congress enacted the National Labor Relations (Wagner) Act
    — Committee for Industrial Organization (CIO) formed within the AFL
1936 — The CIO (renamed the Congress of Industrial Organization) split off from the AFL and, under the leadership of John L. Lewis, became an independent and competing labor federation
    — Labor's Non-Partisan League organized to support President Roosevelt's bid for reelection
1936-37 — The UAW (CIO) conducted a successful sit-down strike against the General Motors Corporation. The GM strike was followed by other sit-downs in auto, such as Chrysler and Hudson, as well as in other establishments of all kinds throughout the state
1943 — War Labor Disputes (Smith-Connally) Act passed
    — CIO-PAC created
1947 — Labor-Management Relations (Taft-Hartley) Act enacted
    — Labor's League for Political Education (AFL) established
1955 — AFL and CIO merged, and the Committee on Political Education (COPE) formed
    — *United States* vs. *UAW* prosecuted
1959 — Congress enacted the Labor-Management Reporting and Disclosure (Landrum-Griffin) Act
1962 — President Kennedy issued Executive Order 10988
    — U.S. Supreme Court issued its opinion in *Baker* vs. *Carr*
    — Michigan Supreme Court decided in favor of one man/one vote principle in *Scholle* vs. *Hare*
1964 — U.S. Supreme Court decided case of *Reynolds* vs. *Sims*
1965 — Public Employment Relations Act (PERA) passed by Michigan Legislature
1968 — The UAW split with the AFL-CIO and, together with the Teamsters, formed the Alliance for Labor Action
1970 — Walter Reuther, president of the UAW, killed in a plane crash; succeeded by Leonard Woodcock

SUGGESTIONS FOR FURTHER READING

No general history of organized labor in Michigan has been published thus far, although books on Michigan history such as the Michigan Writers' Program volume, *Michigan, A Guide to the Wolverine State* (1941), often devote some space to the topic. Nevertheless, much of the information of the kind found in this study must be gathered from a variety of contemporary sources. These include the state labor commissioners' reports, journal and newspaper articles, and the constitutions and by-laws, as well as convention proceedings, of individual unions, the AFL, and the Knights of Labor. Unpublished doctoral dissertations such as Sidney Glazer's "Labor and Agrarian Movements in Michigan, 1876-1896" (The University of Michigan, 1932) and seminar papers on selected aspects of Michigan labor history are also very useful. This kind of material is available in the libraries, particularly in such specialized collections as the Labadie Collection and Michigan Historical Collections at The University of Michigan, the Labor Archives at Wayne State University, and the Burton Collection of the Detroit Public Library. The State Library in Lansing has a good cross-section of the newspapers published in Michigan. These have been microfilmed and are available in that form on interlibrary loan.

GENERAL

There are a number of good one-volume works that deal with American labor history generally, and include many of the highlights of the Michigan story. Among these are Foster Rhea Dulles, *Labor in America* (3d ed., 1966); Henry Pelling, *American Labor* (1960); and Joseph G. Rayback, *A History of American Labor* (1966). All three have very useful bibliographies for those who may wish to delve still further into the history of a particular period in American labor history or investigate a specific subject area. The Rayback list is particularly extensive.

The classic four-volume survey by John R. Commons and associates, *History of Labor in the United States* (1918-1935), should also be consulted. While it takes the story only through 1932, it still remains a mine of information for the years prior to 1932.

In addition to the above, the references given below may also be useful for readers interested in readily available background material relating to the subject matter of the individual chapters.

CHAPTER ONE

Norman J. Ware, *The Industrial Worker, 1840–1860* (1924), emphasizes the impact of industrialism upon the American workers, the various reform schemes that interested them, and particularly their early efforts to achieve the ten-hour day. The same author's *The Labor Movement in the United States, 1860–1895* (1929) contains a detailed history of the Knights of Labor. Ware is very critical of the Knights' long-time Grand Master Workman, Terence Powderley, and to balance that view the reader may also want to look at Powderley's autobiography, *The Path I Trod* (1940), or at George E. McNeill, ed., *The Labor Movement: The Problem of To-Day* (1887). McNeill was himself a Knight and wrote very favorably about the organization and its leaders. Lloyd Ulman, *The Rise of the National Trade Union* (1966), which deals with the emergence of national organizations in the nineteenth century, also has an interesting section on the Knights.

The dual goals of the trade union movement during the period are considered in Gerald Grob, *Workers and Utopia: A Study of the Ideological Conflict in the American Labor Movement, 1865–1900* (1961).

On the rise of the AFL, see Philip Taft, *The A.F. of L. in the Time of Gompers* (1957), and Lewis L. Lorwin and Jean Atherton Flexner, *The American Federation of Labor: History, Policies and Prospects* (1933).

Journal articles of particular interest include Harold C. Brooks, "Story of the Founding of the Brotherhood of Locomotive Engineers," *Michigan History*, 27 (1943), 610–19; Clifton K. Yearley, Jr., "Richard Trevellick: Labor Agitator," *Michigan History*, 39 (1955), 423–44; Albert Blum and Dan Georgakas, "Michigan Labor and the Civil War," Michigan State University School of Labor and Industrial Relations Reprint Series No. 71; and R. C. Stewart, "The Labadie Labor Collection," *Michigan Alumnus Quarterly Review*, 53, No. 20 (Spring 1947), 247–53. The Stewart article contains a short biography of Joseph Labadie, as well as a description of the material in the Collection.

CHAPTER TWO

Vernon Jensen, *Lumber and Labor* (1945), describes labor relations in the lumbering industry generally, and contains a short section on the Saginaw Valley strike. For the background of the strike, see Anita Goodstein, "Labor Relations in the Saginaw Valley Lumber Industry, 1865–1886," *Bulletin of the Business Historical Society*, 27 (1953), 193–221.

CHAPTER THREE

Frank T. Stockton, *The Closed Shop in American Trade Unions* (1911), is the most extensive treatment of the early twentieth century open shop movement. On NAM involvement, see Albion Guilford Taylor, *Labor Policies of the National Association of Manufacturers* (1928). Walter Gordon Merritt, *History of the League for Industrial Rights* (1925), describes the open shop advocates' court battles in detail. Those readers interested in the AFL's early involvement in politics should consult Marc Karson, *American Labor Unions and Politics 1900–1918* (1958), and Mollie Carroll, *Labor and Politics* (1923).

There are numerous journal articles concerning the early twentieth century open shop movement, and references to a wide variety of them can be found in the Stockton, Taylor, and Merritt volumes mentioned above. The reader can get a good idea of the arguments, pro and con, by simply looking through the issues of *The Square Deal* and the *American Federationist* for the period.

CHAPTER FOUR

A good deal has been written on radical unionism in the United States. The works most pertinent for background on radical unionism in the period covered in Chapter Four are David J. Saposs, *Left Wing Unionism* (1926), and William Preston, *Aliens and Dissenters, Federal Suppression of Radicals, 1903–1933* (1963). Vernon H. Jensen, *Heritage of Conflict* (1950), describes labor relations in the nonferrous metal industry to 1930 and has a section on the 1913 strike. Angus Murdoch, *Boom Copper* (1943), has material on the personnel policies of the Michigan copper mining companies, as does William B. Gates, Jr., *Michigan Copper and Boston Dollars, An Economic History of the Michigan Copper Mining Industry* (1951). A journal article on the strike itself is William A. Sullivan, "The 1913 Revolt of the Michigan Copper Miners," *Michigan History*, 43 (1959), 3–23.

CHAPTER FIVE

For the history of labor in the years after World War I and until the advent of the CIO, see Irving Bernstein, *The Lean Years: A History of the American Worker, 1920–1933* (1960), and Philip A. Taft, *The A.F. or L. from the Death of Gompers to the Merger* (1959).

As its subtitle implies, James O. Morris, *Conflict within the A.F. of L.: A Study of Craft versus Industrial Unionism, 1901–1938* (1958), details the developments within the AFL which led to the formation of the CIO.

Irving Bernstein, *The Turbulent Years* (1970), describes the history of organized labor between 1933 and 1941 and contains a long chapter on "The Emergence of the UAW." Walter Galenson, *The C.I.O. Challenge to the A.F. of L.: A History of the American Labor Movement, 1935–1951* (1960), will be of interest to those who wish to know more about the development of the industrial unions affiliated with the CIO. The Galenson volume also has a chapter on the rise of the UAW.

On labor relations in the auto industry specifically, see Sidney Fine, *The Automobile under the Blue Eagle* (1963), and, by the same author, *Sit-Down: The General Motors Strike of 1936–1937* (1969).

Journal articles on auto unionism include Jack W. Skeels, "Early Carriage and Auto Unions: The Impact of Industrialization and Rival Unionism," *Industrial and Labor Relations Review*, 17 (1963–64), 566–83, and two articles by Sidney Fine, "The Tool and Die Makers Strike of 1933," *Michigan History*, 42 (1958), 297–323, and "The Origins of the United Automobile Workers, 1933–1935," *Journal of Economic History*, 18 (1958), 249–282.

CHAPTER SIX

For an overview of labor's role in politics, see Charles M. Rehmus and Doris B. McLaughlin, eds., *Labor and American Politics, A Book of Readings* (1967) Fay Calkins, *The CIO and the Democratic Party* (1952), focuses on the 1950 elections in certain Midwestern states, including Michigan. J. David Greenstone, *Labor in American Politics* (1969), is devoted primarily to a discussion of labor's political activities in Detroit, Chicago, and Los Angeles. Stephen B. and Vera H. Sarasohn, *Political Party Patterns in Michigan* (1957), is the most detailed study of the CIO's entry into politics in Michigan and the subsequent identification of the two major parties with labor and management in the auto industry. The voting behavior of auto workers in the 1952 presidential election is described in Arthur Kornhauser et al., *When Labor Votes, A Study of Auto Workers* (1956.)

Jacqueline Brophy, "The Merger of the AFL and the CIO in Michigan," *Michigan History*, 50 (1966) 139–157, contains information concerning the political obstacles to merging the two federations within the state.

The COPE offices have prepared a number of pamphlets describing the operation of the organization. For example, the manual "How to Win" tells of COPE participation in local elections. That manual, and other similar material, is available through COPE headquarters in Washington.

CHAPTER SEVEN

For public employee unionism in the federal service see Willem B. Vosloo, *Collective Bargaining in the United States* (1966). A sourcebook of pertinent documents on labor organization at all levels of government is Harold S. Roberts, *Labor-Management Relations in the Public Service* (1970). On teacher unionism, see Myron Lieberman and Michael H. Moskow, *Collective Negotiations for Teachers* (1966). Charles M. Rehmus and Evan Wilner, *The Economic Results of Teacher Bargaining: Michigan's First Two Years,* surveys the impact of teacher unionization on school district budgets. The work is Research Paper No. 6 in the Institute of Labor and Industrial Relations (The University of Michigan–Wayne State University) series, published in May 1968. Hyman Parker, *Michigan Public Employment Relations Act and Procedures,* analyzes the provisions of the act in detail. The work is No. 1 (1970) in the Employment Relations Study Series published by Michigan State University's School of Labor and Industrial Relations. Because public employee unionism is currently of such importance, there are a growing number of conference proceedings and journal articles available on the subject. For example, the entire March 1969 issue of the *Michigan Law Review* was devoted to the topic. Changes are taking place so rapidly in the public sector that the *Government Employee Relations Report,* a newsletter issued weekly by the Bureau of National Affairs, should also be consulted.

INDEX

AFL-CIO, 133, 135, 141, 155
agency shop, 154, 160
Alger, Russell, 42–45
Alliance for Labor Action, 133
Alpena (Mich.), 43
Amalgamated Clothing Workers of America, 126
American Anti-Boycott Association, 55, 60
American Bar Association, 150, 151
American Federation of Government Employees, 154
American Federation of Labor (AFL), 26, 50–54, 56, 57, 59–61, 64, 69, 70, 73–76, 86, 97, 99–101, 103–107, 110, 125, 127, 128, 155
American Federation of State, County and Municipal Employees, 154
American Federation of Teachers (AFT), 155, 156
American Federationist, 54, 59, 60
American Motors Corporation, 132
"American Plan," 98. *See also* open shop movement
anarchism and anarchists, 27, 28, 76
"arbitration," as defined in late 19th century, 15
Associated Automobile Workers of America (AAWA), 106, 107
Atlanta (Ga.), *see* General Motors sit-down strikes
Au Sable (Mich.), 43
Auto Workers Union (AWU), 102
Automobile Labor Board (ALB), 105, 106, 109
Automotive Industrial Workers Association (AIWA), 106, 110
automotive industry, in Michigan, 95ff.

Baker Conspiracy Law, 43
Baker vs. *Carr,* 140
Barry, Thomas, 33, 34, 38–40, 43–47
Battle Creek (Mich.), 24, 50, 57, 59, 62, 64–66, 68–73
Battle Creek Citizens' Alliance, 69
Battle Creek *Enquirer,* 70, 71
Battle Creek Industrial Association, 71
Battle Creek Sanitarium, 62, 63, 72
"Battle of the Running Bulls," 113
Bay City (Mich.), 24. *See also* Saginaw Valley strike
Bay County (Mich.), *See* Saginaw Valley strike
Beaskey, John, 36
Beloit (Wis.), 57
Bendix Corporation sit-down strike, 109
bicycle industry, in Michigan, 95
Blinn, D. C., 36, 40, 43, 44
Briggs Manufacturing Company, 102
Brotherhood of Locomotive Engineers (BLE), 9

Michigan National Guard; and copper strike, 78, 83–87; and General Motors
  Flint sit-down strike, 114
Midland Steel Frame Company sit-down strike, 109
militia, in Saginaw Valley strike, 41, 42, 44, 45, 48
Mitchell, John, 86
Monroe (Mich.), 5
Mortimer, Wyndham, 116
Moyer, William, 91, 92
Muncie (Ind.), *see* General Motors strikes
Murphy, Frank, 110, 111, 113–19
Murray Body plant, 102

National Association of Government Employees, 154
National Association of Letter Carriers, 155
National Association of Manufacturers, 55–57, 60, 98, 150
National Council for Industrial Defense, 56, 57, 60
National Education Association, 155, 156
National Industrial Recovery Act (NIRA), 104–06, 109
National Labor Reform Party, 18
National Labor Relations Act, *see* Wagner Act
National Labor Relations Board vs. *Fansteel Metallurgical Corporation,* 121
National Labor Union, 16–19
National Right to Work Committee, 160
National Trades and Workers Association, 70–72
National Typographical Union, 8
New York Times, 43, 94, 119, 126, 135
Nixon, Richard, 132, 151, 160
Norris-LaGuardia Act, 103, 104

Olds Motor Works, 96
Ontonagon County (Mich.), *see* copper strike
open shop movement, 50ff., 98–100. *See also* "right-to-work"
Oscoda (Mich.), 43
Ottawas, 4

Panic of 1837, 7; of 1873, 16, 19
Paw Paw (Mich.), 21
Perkins, Frances, 114
Philadelphia Civil Service Commission, 157
Pinkertons, in Saginaw Valley strike, 41, 44; in copper strike, 85
political action, *see* labor and politics
Political Action Committee (CIO), *see* CIO-PAC
Pontiac (Mich.), 5. *See also* General Motors strikes
Post, C. W., 50, 57ff.
Post Tavern, 68
Post Toasties, 59, 61
Postum, 59, 61, 63, 65

Postum Cereal Company, 58, 59, 63, 64, 68. *See also* C. W. Post
Potawatomi, 4
Powderley, Terence, 47
printers (Detroit), 7, 8
public employee strikes, 145, 148, 149, 151, 158, 159; in Michigan, 145, 148, 149, 151, 153, 163; and compulsory arbitration, 159
public employee unionism, 145ff.; and civil service regulations, 146, 147, 149, 150, 157; and bargaining units, 157, 158; and union security, 160; financial constraints upon, 161–63
Public Employment Relations Act (PERA), 143, 152–54, 162, 163
Pure Food and Drug Act, 63

Rat Gazette, The, 8
reapportionment, 139, 140, 152. *See also Scholle* vs. *Hare*
reform movements, see specific reform cause
Reo Motor Car Company sit-down strike, 120
Republican Party, 123–25, 130–32, 137, 139, 141, 143
Reuther, Roy, 135
Reuther, Walter, 122, 126, 130
Reynolds vs. *Sims,* 141
"right-to-work," 127, 160
Romney, George, 132, 143
Roosevelt, Franklin D., 105, 115, 125–27, 136, 141, 146, 148
Roosevelt, Theodore, 54, 55, 71

Saginaw, Saginaw City, and Saginaw County (Mich.), *see* Saginaw Valley strike, General Motors strikes
Saginaw Valley strike (1885), 29ff.
salt production, in Michigan, 30ff.
Scholle, August, 120, 128, 135, 139. *See also Scholle* vs. *Hare*
Scholle vs. *Hare,* 140, 141
Seeberville (Mich.), 87
Seventh Day Adventists, 62
Shearer, George H., 37, 38, 42
Sherman Antitrust Act, 60, 73
Shiawassee (Mich.), 23n
Ship Carpenters and Caulkers, 14
shoemakers (Detroit), 7
shorter hours movement, 21; *see also* eight- and ten-hour movements
sit-down strikes, 108ff. *See also* individual companies
Sloan, Alfred P., Jr., 114
Smith, Al, 126n
Smith-Connally (War Labor Disputes) Act, 136, 137
socialism and Socialists, 13, 22, 23, 51, 76, 79, 80, 122
Socialist Labor Party, 22
Socialist Party, 79

Waddell, James, 85. *See also* Mahon-Waddell Corporation
Wagner Act, 106, 112, 120, 127, 153
Wagner, Robert F., 151
Wallace, George, 132, 133
Wallace, Henry, 129
Washington Literary Society, 23
welfare capitalism, 56, 57; and C. W. Post, 65–68; in the Copper Country, 77, 78, 80, 81; in the auto industry, 98, 99
Western Federation of Miners (WFM), 75, 76, 79ff.
Western Federation of Miners women's auxiliary, 91
white-collar workers, 147*n*, 163, 164
War of 1812, 3
Williams, G. Mennen, 129, 130, 132
Wilson, Charles E., 131
Wolman, Leo, 61
Workingman's Advocate, The, 10–12
World War I, 73, 94
World War II, 149
Wyandotte (Mich.), 95

"yellow-dog" contracts, 56, 104
YMCA (Detroit), 100
Yorkville (Mich.), 64
Ypsilanti Workingmen's Society, 5